MARKINGS

of Mercy

THE STORY OF AFTER
ABORTION HELPLINE

JOAN PENDERGAST

DENVER, COLORADO

would be helpful — there is a need — community Maternity Services

Mission Statement

Nobody wants to think about abortion, especially how harmful it is. So we deny, deny, deny. So many people are suffering. For every aborted child there are two parents affected, four grandparents, other relatives and friends. We can help.

I wrote this book to help people think about the effects of abortion on so many in our world. In the process I've revealed a lot about my own life for a couple of reasons. Though I have not had an abortion, I've dealt with sudden grief and guilt since I was seven years of age, when my mother collapsed right next to me and died shortly thereafter. I thought her death was my fault. While recovering from that pain many years later, I started thinking about women and men trying to recover from the devastation of an abortion. In reaching out I was healed. I thought my story might draw others into considering the reality of post-abortion problems, through the events that drew me into starting a post-abortion telephone helpline.

This book may be a small contribution in light of all the amazing efforts of others to bring the truth of abortion to light, but it is my way of helping people recover from the after-effects of abortion. I have shared what I know so others can heal and help their relatives, friends or acquaintances who choose to share their pain. My hope is that they can find healing for their wounds and hope for their future.

Table of Contents

MISSION STATEMENT iii

INTRODUCTION vii

THE GOSPEL OF LIFE xi

ACKNOWLEDGMENTS xvii

CHAPTER I... 1
  FRIENDS PRAYING 1
  DECEMBER 19, 1943...2
  RIGHT AFTER MOM'S DEATH..............................6
  NEW FAMILY 10
  THE CRUCIFIX 13
  COURTSHIP, COLLEGE, MARRIAGE.................15
  MARRIED LIFE...23
  PRAYER MEETINGS 26
  UNFINISHED BUSINESS - ABOUT MOM.............30

CHAPTER II 33
  HOMEWARD BOUND - DAD...............................33
  HARVARD HEARS A MOTHER'S PLEA 38
  THREADS OF MERCY...42
  YOU WERE CREATED IN AN EXPLOSION OF LOVE ...42
  POST-ABORTION MARKINGS OF MERCY 44
  I HATE CHRISTIANS 44
  LIKE A CUP OF COFFEE 47
  COURAGE..49
  INTO THE HEART OF A DOOMED LAND 51
  1983: POPE JOHN PAUL II AND THE HOLY YEAR OF

REDEMPTION 53
ON THE SCRAP HEAP, 1983 55
NOVENA 56

CHAPTER III 58
TESTING THE HUNCH 58
ARTICLES AND STORIES..................................62

CHAPTER IV 70
THE DEVELOPMENT AND BIRTH OF AFTER
ABORTION HELPLINE, INC. 70

CHAPTER V.. 80
CALLERS..80
NARRATIVES FROM CALL SHEETS....................82

CHAPTER VI... 92
CONFERENCES: A TURNING POINT 92
REFERRALS...94
AT PEACE 96
SECOND RHODE ISLAND CONFERENCE.............97

CHAPTER VII 100
PROJECT RACHEL 100
RACHEL'S VINEYARD 102
TRANSITION...103
IF YOU WANT TO HELP A FRIEND 104
THE VOCABULARY OF FEELINGS......................106
LIST OF POST-ABORTION REACTIONS 107
JULIE...108
FULL CIRCLE...109

EPILOGUE: A CALLING.................................. 111

BIBLIOGRAPHY 114

Introduction

The reality of post-abortion suffering is denied or ignored by many people and by most of the news media. Denying this reality doesn't mean it does not exist. It is no wonder there is so much denial. So many people have been party to one or more abortions, and each one can be a devastating event.

For the last twenty-five years I have been helping women and men recover from the trauma of abortion. The reality of this pain dawned on me gradually. In a beautiful way God, who loves us all, began to show me the pain at my son's graduation from Harvard University, on June 10, 1982. Mother Teresa of Calcutta, who received an honorary degree at the graduation, showed me the way. Her presence and prayers were a source of God's grace for all of us. At the Class Day speech she had spoken bravely about the love we owe one another. She had said "love until it hurts." On that day I began to see that people suffering after abortion suffer from a kind of pain that mirrors the deepest pain in my own life, my mother's sudden death when I was seven. For years I believed that her death was my fault. Grief, loss and guilt were my constant companions.

As I sat in that audience, I wondered, "There are people here who might be able to understand me and my pain. And maybe, just maybe I can understand them." I felt a new calling: I had to follow the course of connecting with people suffering and troubled after abortion. The first part of this story is meant to trace the events in my life that led me to that point of challenge. The second part is about helping people recover from abortion. I chose the title **Markings of Mercy** because I see these life events or markings, as just that, God's loving mercy for me. "God's mercy is everlasting" (Daniel 3). In a way, the first section, which summarizes the early parts of my life, is praise to God for being so merciful to me.

God's mercy sums up what we all need during difficult times, individually and collectively as a people. In many cases, this involves those who sanction abortions and have abortions. I think most people do not know or want to know what abortion is doing to women and men, their families and friends. Perhaps they wouldn't know, out of ignorance or inexperience, how to handle the pain. Then too, there is such a riptide out there trying to prove it's a good thing for women.

Perhaps people do not realize how merciful God is. Perhaps they do not know Jesus Christ, true God and true man, and His loving, truthful ways. Perhaps a friendship with Jesus Christ seems a distant hope for others.

Because I believe Jesus Christ is merciful, forgiving and Love itself, I have hope for people suffering after abortion. Jesus said:

"The spirit of the Lord is upon me;
therefore, he has anointed me.
He has sent me to bring glad tidings to the poor,
to proclaim liberty to captives,
Recovery of sight to the blind
and release to prisoners,
To announce a year of favor from the Lord."

(Luke 4, v 18,19)

Jesus, God's chosen one in whom God is pleased,

"shall bring forth justice to the nations,
Not crying out, not shouting,
not making his voice heard in the street.
A bruised reed he shall not break,
and a smoldering wick he shall not quench."

(Isaiah 42, v 3)

My hope in Christ enabled me to write this story, to share these little vignettes and information. I hope that others might be encouraged by my story to find healing and to help others find healing. My journey resulted in After Abortion Helpline, a free, non-sectarian, and anonymous telephone service staffed by trained, compassionate volunteers, willing to listen and help people troubled after abortion who would call the Helpline. I have described its planning and development with a two-fold purpose. One is to tell its story. And, more importantly, to help others prepare to reach out to someone in their lives who is troubled after abortion. The newspaper articles about conferences and programs we've conducted are meant also to educate and enable readers to help others. I have tried to pass on as much as I could.

Many of the names, dates, places and times related in this book have been changed to protect the identities of the persons involved.

THE GOSPEL OF LIFE

PARAGRAPH # 99

"I would now like to say a special word to women who have had an abortion. The church is aware of the many factors which may have influenced your decision, and she does not doubt that, in many cases, it was a painful and even shattering decision. The wound in your heart may not yet have healed. Certainly what happened was and remains terribly wrong. But do not give in to discouragement and do not lose hope. Try rather to understand what happened and face it honestly. If you have not already done so, give yourselves over with humility and trust to repentance. The Father of mercies is ready to give you his forgiveness and his peace in the sacrament of reconciliation. You will come to understand that nothing is definitively lost, and you will also be able to ask forgiveness from your child, who is now living in the Lord. With the friendly and expert help and advice of other people and as a result of your painful experience, you can be among the most eloquent defenders of everyone's right to life. Through your commitment to life, whether by accepting the birth of other children or by welcoming and caring for those most in need of someone to be close to them, you will become promoters of a new way of looking at human life."

Pope John Paul II,
Evangelium Vitae, The Gospel of Life, paragraph 99

"All my hope lies solely in your mercy."
St. Augustine
Confessions, 10

"There is no greater love than this:
to lay down one's life for one's friends."
John 15:13
On the World War I monument in
Edgemont Park, Montclair, New Jersey

"Mercy is not an idea, but a Person: Jesus Christ."
Father Richard Veras

For the Glory of God
And For The Good Of Souls

For Jack
My very good husband of fifty-three years,
who helped me understand
my story and loved me through it.

ACKNOWLEDGMENTS

Many people contributed to this story - too many to mention them all. A big thank you goes to everyone who has helped me in any way.

Thanks to my daughter, Joan, who, when she was a college writing tutor, supported and instructed me to "write through the pain," for Chapter I. "I'll be here but you have to write it," she said.

Thanks to Pat Fogarty, writer and friend, for getting me started. When she interviewed me on TV for the Helpline, I knew she understood our mission. Pat helped me write the book's first draft.

Thanks to my sister Susu who edited the story of Mom's suffering and death.

Thanks to Biddy B. who many years later said: "Send me a manuscript in ten days and I will read it for you." She made me scramble to put one together and gave me wonderful encouragement and suggestions.

Thanks to Connie, Isabelle, Wendy, Pat O'D., Diane H., Mary R., Pila, Sally, Kelly, Sue and others who helped with suggestions and prayed me through to the end.

Thanks to Jack, my patient editor, of the first complete manuscript, and several since. And thanks to Francesca, my dear friend, who dropped everything to edit the final draft.

Thanks to my granddaughters Maddy, Max, and also Gus who had just arrived at my home for a visit. Upon being asked to move my book manuscript off the dining room table so we could eat lunch, they said: "Book, what book?" and proceeded to read it out loud to me all afternoon. Thanks to them for their delight and encouraging comments.

Thanks to Judy Costa, my post-abortion co-worker, my first "reader," for encouragement and valuable corrections.

Thanks to Diane Manning, my second "reader," for her valuable suggestions and for her friendship and wisdom as we built After Abortion Helpline.

Thanks to my son, John, my third "reader," for his great suggestions, loving comments, and patient computer help.

Thanks to several close friends and relatives who read this story and gave me their honest opinions.

Thanks to all our generous donors to the Helpline, of varied religious beliefs and backgrounds. Thanks for encouraging, sustaining and praying for us, for twenty-five years.

Thanks to Helen A. who called me when the Helpline opening was written up in The Providence Journal and said: "Someone had to come up with this idea. I'm glad it was you."

Thanks to Richard Dujardin, our incredible religion writer for The Providence Journal, who did such a beautiful job reporting on our Helpline activities.

For everyone mentioned in this book, my love and deep gratitude.

Last but not least, I am deeply grateful to everyone who served on the Board of Directors and on the Helpline, as telephone volunteers. They are beautiful warriors of love in this healing work

And, deep gratitude to each caller who had the grace and courage to reach out for help and called us on the Helpline. Bless you all.

MARKINGS
of Mercy

Chapter I

One day, almost forty years ago, my doorbell rang. My friend, Jane, was at the door. I invited her in and we sat down in my living room to visit. Jane began our conversation with: "I have something to tell you. A few months ago I went to another country and had an abortion."

This was the first time anyone told me they had an abortion. I didn't know anything about what goes on in an induced abortion. I knew "abortion" as a word for a very early miscarriage. But here I was with this dear woman who was explaining to me what she did.

I just prayed silently for the grace to be a loving friend. I don't remember the rest of our conversation, but I do remember my heart was filled with love for Jane.

This visit has been with me all these years.

FRIENDS PRAYING

I'm not sure exactly when this story began. I believe it began sometime in God's heart. But I will begin this book with a beautiful, hot clear August afternoon in 1986. My friends Anne, Mary, and Cathy were sitting with me in white lawn chairs in Mary's backyard, a few houses back from the sparkling ocean at Sakonnet Harbor, in Rhode Island. We were gathered to visit and pray together. Seagulls soared above us to and fro, in their constant hunt for food. Little song birds sang in the trees. Red geraniums in big pots decorated the yard, and orange daylilies swayed sedately in the cool breeze. Blue hydrangea bushes dotted the yard. It was a luscious spot to enjoy with good friends.

I had just returned from the National Post Abortion Conference called **Healing Visions**, in South Bend, Indiana. As I shared about it, Cathy, who is also a nurse, said: "Your enthusiasm is wonderful. You understand so much about abortion and what it does to people, but you are way ahead of me. I just had to put some puppies to sleep and I still don't know how I feel about it. I've got very mixed feelings and I can't figure them out. Losing a child through abortion is much more complex to deal with. There must be some real sorting out to do, even some healing. I'm trying to work it through and they were only puppies. I don't understand much about healing after abortion but I really want to. I know you've been thinking hard about this for a long time. Write down your beginnings before you forget them. That could help us."

"Make it a process story so we can do our own processing," Cathy continued. "Our Congregational church just went through months of processing together deciding whether or not to allow the *Witches of Eastwick* to be filmed in our colonial church. It took us ages to decide not to, but the process our congregation experienced was invaluable. Going through all that searching helped us understand our personal issues. It was hard work but well worth the effort."

As Cathy spoke, my heart was leaping with joy. The story she was asking for had been building in my head and heart for some time. I needed Cathy's boost to get it going on paper. I woke up at 6:30 the next morning and began putting this story together.

DECEMBER 19, 1943

"Mummy, are you going to die?" I ask. At seven years old I have to know.

Her eyes flutter open. Her two sapphire blue eyes flash at me beneath her weak lids.

It is the week before Christmas, 1943. Holly and new baby bouquets decorate our house in New Jersey. Two weeks ago, Mummy finally brought our new baby sister, Heather, home, our Thanksgiving baby, arriving home just before Christmas.

Mom's been in bed since then with lumbago of the back, whatever that is. Today Mummy, Daddy and I are going to our Congregational Church to hear me sing in the children's choir. Mom and I are getting dressed together in her bedroom.

She is so beautiful. Her tall, soft, warm, cuddly body makes me feel safe as we stand there, the two of us, combing our hair in front of the mirror. She is reaching for her lipstick in a drawer in her huge mahogany bureau, which is covered with all kinds of treasures: a secret penny box, an atomizer, a box of powder, a silver brush and comb, and some jewelry.

Suddenly she sways, grasping for the drawer, and crashes to the floor, yelling out my father's name, "Shaw!"

I dive to the floor where she is lying. My eyes are glued to her face waiting for a sign, waiting for a chance to ask her what is happening. I cannot understand what is going on. Daddy rushes in from the bathroom, his face covered with white foam. Bending down beside her, he calls "Joan." Again he calls her name but she does not answer him. He reaches in her lipstick drawer for a vial of smelling salts. He snaps it and puts it under her nose. She does not move.

"Stay here," he says to me. "I am going to call Doctor Meeker." He runs to the telephone downstairs. I am alone with my mother.

"Wake up Mummy. Wake up," I say. She does not move. I try again moving closer to her face so she can hear me better. **"Wake up Mummy...please...PLEASE. MUMMY. MUMMY. MUMMY-Y-Y.** My eyes sting. "Big girl don't cry," I tell myself. Kneeling down, crouched down, I glue my eyes to her eyelids. She will hear me now, I know. "Mummy," I keep calling over and over again.

She did. Suddenly her eye lids flutter and then they open...they are wide-eyed, staring right at me. Quickly, before she goes back to sleep, I ask her, "Mummy, are you going to die?" Now we are talking like we always do, asking questions and getting answers. She answers and says: "No Dear. Of course not, I am not going to die."

Oh no. She went to sleep again. Oh no. Mummy… Mummy.

Daddy and Mrs. Struckman, the baby nurse, come into the room. They hurry over to us. "We are going to put Mummy in her bed now," Daddy says to me. Together they put her there, under the covers.

"I'm here," Dr. Meeker announces, as he races up the stairs into the bedroom. Daddy must have left the front door open for him. The doorbell did not ring. He goes to my mother's side and begins to check her out while Daddy says to me: "Pixie, get Bruce and go play downstairs." As I leave the room, he closes the door behind me.

I find my younger brother, Bruce. "Something awful has happened to Mummy," I try to explain. "She fell on the floor and she won't wake up."

We go to Mummy's door and try to listen to what's happening. We hear her snoring…then there are other kinds of sounds, quite loud. It doesn't really sound like Mummy but it is *her* voice. I'm scared. "We'd better go downstairs like Daddy said," I tell Bruce. I feel bad standing here by the door. I am not supposed to be here. Something awful is happening. I can't stand it.

We scurry down the stairs, head for the kitchen and close the door. It is safe here. We cannot hear those awful sounds any more. We should not have stayed so long. Bruce and I wait for Daddy. Bruce is five and I am seven.

I hear the kitchen door open and Daddy's footsteps slowly come to where we are. He bends down and puts one arm around each of us. He looks at each of us as he says our names. His eyes are sad. He is very serious. "Children, your Mummy has just died. She is gone. She will not come back again."

We huddle on the kitchen floor. I dissolve in tears. My brother stands there wide-eyed, watching.

Bruce and I stay in the kitchen while Daddy does some things. I cannot stop crying. I hurt all over. Daddy comes to us. He tells us, "We are going to Grandmary and Grandpa's house now." They are my Daddy's parents. Mummy's parents died the year before I was born.

"Dry your tears and wash your face and hands," he says. I am already dressed in my Sunday clothes.

We leave our house and Mrs. Struckman and the baby. We get in the car and drive to the big brown house on Belleview Avenue, my other home. "Oh good" I think. "Isabelle and Hazel will be there. I can play in the kitchen with them. Maybe Isabelle will have some almond custard in the ice box." "Grandpa always tickles me the minute I get inside the door. I giggle so much it's hard to run away but I always do."

I picture Grandmary sitting in her big wing chair in front of the living room window that has curtains you can sort of see through. When Mummy, Bruce and I visit her after school at four o'clock, we have tea. Not us kids, though. We drink grape juice and ginger ale through silver straws. It tastes so good. It gives me something to do while the grown-ups talk on and on. Grown ups. *Mummy, oh no. She is not here.*

I'm trying to keep myself from making too much noise as I walk up the big front steps. Grandpa doesn't tickle me this time. He hugs me tight. We burst out crying. Then I go to Grandmary whose eyes are red and puffy. "It's all right, dear. I know it hurts. You may cry," she says.

There are other people there. They are all grown-ups. They all talk softly. I go around and hug these big people. My aunts and uncles are there and some white-haired friends of Grandmary's. In the dining room I see Isabelle and Hazel putting food and things on the table. I run to Isabelle for a hug. She doesn't speak. She just hugs, tears rolling down her face. Then pretty Hazel, Isabelle's daughter, holds me tight. "I am sorry that your mother died," she says. "Your Mommy was a special lady and you are too. It won't be the same without her, but you'll be alright, honey, don't you worry. We will be right here. And we will have custard in the icebox whenever you come."

Quick...I need to get away. They make me happy but that hurt is back again. It comes and goes but when it comes I feel all crazy like I don't know what will happen. I find a corner in the front hall just outside the dining room where nobody can see me, or hear the awful sounds I make.

I hear my name. A grown up is talking about me. "Pixie wore her mother out," I hear her say. I try to breathe through all the gunk in my head. Is it my fault all this is happening? If it is, I've never been in this much trouble before.

I think back. *We were getting dressed together. Mummy was going out for the first time. She was going out because of me, to hear me sing in the church children Christmas choir. She didn't have to go. It would have been O.K. Then she fell. I tried to wake her up, but she still died. I was with her. It's all my fault. I wore her out. I made her die.*

I don't tell anyone this. I leave the corner and walk very slowly toward the dining room table. Carefully I pull out a chair, and slip into the seat. I am hungry. The pancakes taste good, but since I'm soaked in tears and all mixed up, it's hard to swallow. I pick away and watch the grown-ups eat.

RIGHT AFTER MOM'S DEATH

I don't know when I stopped crying.

Mom was buried. I didn't get to go. I didn't see her in the funeral home either. Daddy said she looked awful and he didn't want me to see her that way. She was cremated and Daddy told me her ashes were put in her favorite vase that had been on the mantle piece. I think I remember it. During the funeral I made Christmas cookies with a very nice family from church.

One of the daughters had been in the play 'The Secret Garden', which Mom took me to. She was very beautiful and I kind of idolized her, so it felt special to be making cookies with her. But the pain wouldn't go away.

I never saw my mother again.

We had Christmas. Years later, my Aunt Mary told me Mom left presents all wrapped up for us. Aunt Mary had come to help Daddy take care of us. I do not remember that. I do remember the Betsy Wetsy Doll my Grandfather gave me, as he did every Christmas. It was wonderful to play with her.

I stayed out of school for a long time, a month or so. It was first grade, Mrs. Leibold's class. When I got back, everyone was very nice to me.

My Dad got me into ballet class at school but I got stomachaches so I quit that for tap dancing, which my friends were taking. I don't think I danced very long. I was in Brownies, too, then Girl Scouts after school. Our elementary school put on the play, *Heidi,* and I was in it in some capacity.

I don't know what I was like, how I seemed to others in those days, but I do know my Dad was wonderful to me. He really took care of me. I felt close to him. He was there for us even though he worked very hard in New York City as a water works engineer each day, taking the train in from our home in Montclair, New Jersey. I knew my Dad loved me. He gave us his office telephone number and promised we could call him if we needed to. We did.

And my Aunt Celie, Mom's sister, was like a mother to me. She lived in town. I played at her house a lot with my cousin, Wayne, who was my age. Wayne made model airplanes all the time and I watched him, fascinated. We lived next door to each other until the year before Mom died, so we were like brother and sister. We grew up together.

At some point Mrs. Donovan, we called her Donna, came to care for us. My Dad found her through business friends. Her husband was in a Veteran's Hospital in Brooklyn, New York. Donna brought her daughter Tina, Tina's four-year-old daughter, Judy, and their dog, Captain Midnight (Cappy for short), to live with us. Tina's husband was overseas in the army.

During their stay, some of their relatives bought a home uptown and they'd go visit often and take us there sometimes. I remember a boy my age named Richard who lived there.

One evening they left for a party there. I stayed home with Bruce and my baby sister, Heather. We'd all been put to bed. I think my dad was on a business trip. I wanted to go to the party. So, I got dressed, left home, took the bus uptown and arrived at the party. I don't recall if they left the party and went back home with me or not. It's creepy to think about this now---that I would just take off like that. And who was taking care of us? We were seven, five and under one year old.

Tina and Donna used to have coffee with cupcakes. Often I'd go to the store at Watchung Plaza on my bike (it had been Mom's), and buy them Hostess cupcakes with a squiggle of white frosting across the top.

Sometimes on those errands I'd stop in at the drug store to shop with pennies I stole from Mom's secret penny box. The box was on her bureau and it opened in a secret way: you slid the front top forward and pulled it up. Her supply of pennies was ample for me to buy candy and greeting cards with tiny plastic beads that made them sparkle and shimmer. I liked those cards. I probably gave them to Donna and Tina.

I obviously had pretty free rein during those days.

My baby sister drank milk from a bottle so I used to make Jello and put it in a bottle when it was warm liquid and take it to bed. I sucked my thumb for a long time.

One day I took my baby sister in the carriage with little Judy holding on. We went for a walk, in Edgemont Park, a block from our house. There was a huge pond in it. It seemed like a good idea to walk close to the water's edge so we did and Judy tripped and fell in a little. When we got home, her mother saw her wet clothes and asked me what happened. Do you believe I said, "Oh a cloud passed over us and it rained on Judy and got her wet." I don't remember what they said. But I did not get yelled at for lying.

TINA'S DEATH

Donna and Tina and Judy and Cappy stayed with us for a while. But this came to an abrupt end, as I recall, after the tragic event of Tina's death. She was getting a little house in Pompton Lakes, New Jersey, ready for her husband's return from the war, and one day she stayed there, waiting for the gas company man to hook up the stove.

Bruce and I skated after school on Edgemont Pond where Daddy was to pick us up and take us to get Tina at her house. We were going to stop for a hamburger, a big treat, on the way home. It was scary, though. I sensed something was wrong as I skated. It was a dismal foreboding of some kind.

Sure enough, when we got to Tina's house and Daddy went in to get her, he didn't come back to the car for a long time. When Daddy came out, he told us Tina was dead from a gas leak. Amazingly, it felt kind of normal. Someone dies and you go through it. You deal with it in a regular sort of way. This time I knew it was not my fault like when my mother died. Tina was Judy's mother. Judy lived with her own mother at our house. Her family was helping us out. Now little Judy was a "half orphan" too, like me.

I think Donna and Judy left to be with family and Judy's dad came home. I don't remember more than that.

My dad was the one most constant figure in my life. I do remember, even before Tina died and her family left us, that after Church on Sundays, my Dad took Bruce, Wayne and me to the Wedgewood Cafeteria for Sunday dinner and then we'd go to the movies. We saw Bambi, whose mother dies, so I cried and cried. We saw many Lassie movies, and the last one got Wayne and me crying so much that we had to leave the theater. That was the end of our movie treats. My dad said we wouldn't be going any more since they made us so sad.

During the week Bruce and I would have our supper of cold cereal at 5:00 p.m., lying on the living room floor, listening to radio serials like Tom Mix, Jack Armstrong and Sky King.

My Aunt Celie, Wayne's mother and Mom's sister, was the person most like my Mom. I could pretend a little bit that she was my Mom. I'd often ask her to tell us stories about when she and Mom were little and she told us lots of wonderful stories. This made me feel good.

I didn't know anyone whose mother had died. I don't remember talking with anyone about Mom's death. I had plenty of companionship in my grief...my whole family, my grandparents, my aunts and uncles, my cousins, and Isabelle and Hazel. I was sure we all missed Mom. Just thinking about how much I missed her all the time brings tears to my eyes. I tried to be as normal as possible through all this. In fact, at times I was even relieved that my mother had only died---actually relieved that she and my Dad were not divorced. I missed my mom all the time.

My Mom had lots of friends. As I grew older, they would often stop me at parties to say how wonderful she was, how they knew her, how kind she was. I had this host of people who made sure I knew my Mom was a great lady, loved and admired and not forgotten. These people were way stations of strength for me. I carried these comments with me in my heart and memory. They were golden identity threads connecting me to Mom, my real mother, my flesh and blood mother whom I knew for seven years. I always knew my Dad loved me.

In June, Daddy drove Bruce, Heather and me to our summer cottage in Rhode Island. It took seven hours and included two short ferry boat rides. When Mom was alive, before my sister was born, we went to Rhode Island on the overnight Fall River Line Ferry. I think this was to save gas during the war. It was a ton of fun for Bruce and me, sleeping in bunk beds, throwing our slippers up and down at each other.

NEW FAMILY

And then one evening my Dad sat us down and said, "I have good news for you. How would you like to have three new sisters, Cessie, Prissy, and Susu? Their mom, Vivian and I, are planning to be married in August!"

Vivian Guerin had recently lost her husband. She was a childhood friend of my Mom's and she and her three daughters were our next door neighbors at the shore. Francesca was my age and Priscilla and Suzanna were younger.

The wedding took place on August 3, 1946, in the church sacristy of Notre Dame des Victoires, Vivian's Catholic parish in Woonsocket, Rhode Island, and dinner followed at my new Grandmother Guerin's house. It was fun. It was funny when my Dad had trouble getting the wedding ring on his new wife's finger. Someone had to get soap from the kitchen so it would slip on.

We waved goodbye to them as they drove away to their honeymoon in the White Mountains in New Hampshire, and a twinge of sadness tugged at me. There goes my Dad, I thought. Now I have to share him with four new people.

That first year was tough for everybody. One sister hemorrhaged after having her tonsils out. Another sister had nervous stomach problems and had trouble eating, and I was hospitalized with an abscess on my ankle. They put me on penicillin shots every three hours, lanced the abscess in the operating room and stuffed it with drains. I was hospitalized for three or four weeks. I became allergic to the penicillin and broke out in huge hives all over my body.

My Dad came to see me most every evening. That made me feel very happy and secure.

When I came home I had to stay in bed a lot. Grandmary Cole brought me flowers, a portable record player and a John Phillip Souza record of marches. On subsequent visits she brought me Louisa May Alcott books to read.

I was very lucky to have an older friend next door. Trudy was engaged to be married and she was very beautiful, but she had the mumps and had to stay in bed too. Her room was across the driveway from mine and we wrote each other notes and drew each other pictures.

The doctors didn't know if I had rheumatic fever, osteomyelitis or something else, but I recovered. My experience made me think about becoming a nurse someday. Maybe I could help people too. Grandmary's father and brother were doctors. In fact, her brother, Dr. John Rockwell, helped invent the X-Ray machine which cost him a finger or two. We saw him often. I liked him a lot.

Eventually we all recovered from our ailments and the next summer the three oldest girls Francesca ("Cessie"), Priscilla ("Prissy") and I went to Camp Wohelo, a summer camp in Maine. We were put in different cabins so we had our own circle of friends and our own lives there. I remember thinking it was cool having these friends also as sisters, members of my family. Less than a year separated each of us. Cessie, the oldest, was five months older than I and I was eleven months older than Prissy. We went to that camp for many summers and two of us went on to become counselors there. I remember coming home to our summer house after camp and nobody our age knew who we were or that we had done great activities and accomplished great things at camp.

While we were at camp in Maine that first summer, our New Jersey house was redecorated and enlarged a little with a longer living room and above it a new bedroom and bath for my parents. It wasn't finished in time for school so we slept at the houses of different relatives and friends for some weeks. I stayed at our friends, the Straights, and I remember ripping the bed sheet with my toes and feeling very guilty about it. I also remember being terrified by their dog. They were very nice people and their son was a great singer at Amherst College. This impressed me. Mrs. Straight had been a good friend of my "real Mom."

Our new home was lovely. We each had our own bedroom. Gone was the wallpaper covered with cherries that my "real Mom" gave me, and my old corner room next to Trudy's house. Now my room was at the opposite end of the hall in a different corner of the house.

New Mom, real Mom, which is Mom? Who is my Mom? Where is my Mom? Oh brother. I got confused a lot about this. I had a divided loyalty. My Real Mom was truly my Mom, but she wasn't there anymore. I missed her all the time, but I had to "get with the program" and get busy building this new blended family. My Dad was counting on me. I had to help him out. It was my job. He asked me to be exceptionally nice and helpful to my new mother. We were not to use the word "step" for our family EVER. Our parents told us they loved each of us equally, as much as they loved their own three children. Since each of us had lost a parent or spouse, I figured we were all in the same boat together. I was sure we six kids felt the same grief and loss. I just assumed this. We didn't talk about it. Basic facts like the dramatic story of the fatal accident of my stepsisters' father were described, as were memories their mother had of my mother. The two mothers had lived two streets away from each other growing up. But deep matters of grief and sorrow were to be kept private. I assumed everyone was feeling the same things I was, more or less.

So, *walk gently* was my motto and don't rock the boat; everyone here is in pain from losing someone.

THE CRUCIFIX

My new sisters used to go to confession on Saturday afternoons, so I went with them. We walked uptown to St. Cassian's Church, half an hour by foot. They asked if I could go to confession and the priest said no, so I waited for them in a pew up front. When I settled down and looked all around, there was a lot to see. There was a box on the altar called the Tabernacle where my sisters told me Jesus was there alive, in the form of Holy Bread. There was a lit sanctuary candle nearby in red glass saying that Jesus was there. As I sat there looking around, in front I saw a big Crucifix with Jesus hanging on it. It was beautiful, unlike crosses I was used to seeing without Jesus' body on them. I kept looking and looking and thinking and, I guess, talking to Jesus quietly. "You suffered a lot. You probably understand the pain I have deep down inside of me from my mother dying. The people in this church aren't afraid of seeing your pain. Maybe they wouldn't be afraid of my pain. I can't really talk about it anywhere. Maybe it's O.K. here."

I kept this to myself. It made me feel better. Perhaps I wasn't alone after all.

RELIGION

In 1937 at the age of eight months, I had been 'dedicated' at the First Universalist Church, along with my two cousins, on my mother's side, in Woonsocket, Rhode Island, where my mother grew up. My Dad and his parents were Congregationalists, and I grew up in their Church in New Jersey. I was active in the youth group where I played hymns on the piano for our services, sang in the young people's choir, went on trips to Washington in the spring and had some nice friends. I enjoyed myself and have warm memories of those times. They were good, nice people--my Dad's people, and I felt comfortable with them.

Seminarians from Union Theological Seminary in New York City would come out to lead our Sunday evening youth group sessions. I don't remember much of what we did, but I do remember questioning a couple of seminarians about our beliefs. I didn't receive any clear answers: "Well, this depends on" or "some say this and some say that." Years earlier I had heard my new sister, Susu, memorizing her catechism out loud and it made sense to me to have beliefs you could be sure of.

One day during those years, I asked my "new mother" if she would teach me about the Catholic faith, to which she replied: "No, I can't do that but you could go see a priest and talk to him about that." I didn't press it because I realized her instructing me could create division in our new blended family. Half of us were Congregationalists and half were Catholic. We each went our separate ways for both worship and religious education. The Catholics went to Catholic school. The Protestants went to public school until we all ended up attending private schools for high school. We did all pray grace before meals together but we never "discussed" religion that I recall.

I waited until I left home for college to see a Catholic priest for instruction in the Catholic faith.

JUNIOR HIGH SCHOOL

My brother and I attended George Innis Junior High School. We played in the school orchestra. Bruce played the bassoon and I played the piano.

I went on to the Kimberley School, a private girl's high school in Montclair. I had begged my father to let me go to the public high school, but he refused. "You'd want to spend time having fun with your friends instead of studying," he said, and he was right.

My concentration wasn't all it might have been. Missing my Mom and having another one tugged at me inside. It was always in the back of my thoughts and emotions. I struggled to do my homework. Reading was somewhat difficult. I thought about my friends, boys and the next fun thing to do outside.

I'd always heard my Mom's friends meant everything to her and that she was generous and kind to them. Once she got flowers from someone, and we delivered them right away to a sick friend. Mom had many Junior League meetings at our house. She wrote funny stories for their magazine, "The League's Latest", of which she was editor. They all did a lot for the World War II effort.

My grades were alright but my parents thought they were not good enough for me to play after-school sports. I was naturally athletic, though, as were my "Real Mom" and Dad, but I was not an intellectual. My friends meant more to me than anything and I went to high school with some wonderful girls. I also had two cousins my age, Wayne and Bob, with whom I'd grown up and this helped enlarge my circle of friends.

School, church and home were at the center of my life. The family was a busy place and church youth group and young people's choir kept me busy and productive. Our town, a New Jersey suburb of New York City, was sheltered, safe and traditional. Many fathers, including my own, worked in New York and commuted by train.

COURTSHIP, COLLEGE, MARRIAGE

Our first encounter with each other was across the aisle in the General Store in Raymond, Maine. Jack was a counselor at Camp Timanous, a boy's camp on Panther Pond, and I was a counselor from Camp Wohelo in South Casco, on Sebago Lake. Jack and I had each brought our Catholic campers to the general store after Mass on Sunday. We purchased newspapers and supervised campers filling orders for candy and junk food. I was sixteen, he was seventeen. It was July, 1953.

We had both eyed each other in church, of course, but we didn't speak at the store. Only our eyes met. He was sure I was a nice Catholic girl, which I wasn't. I assumed he was a nice Catholic guy. But to me he was much more than that. I was in awe of him. He was tall and handsome. He had a presence that snowed me. Nevertheless, that was our meeting, so to speak. I didn't think much more about him because I liked another guy.

Then one evening he joined us on the bluff overlooking Lake Sebago, down the road from camp, where on our evenings off a big group of counselors drank beer and sang songs for a couple of hours. We couldn't go to the movies, they were too far away, nor to dances, as we had early curfew. We had to go far enough away so we wouldn't wake up the campers. Sometimes we played cards, or read or chatted in the rec. cabin. Anyway there he was, with us, without his girlfriend. I thought he was rather nice, even though I was with Dave, my boyfriend from his camp.

As the summer wore on, Dave wrote me a "Dear Joan" letter explaining how he wasn't really in love with me. It was just a good letter, well put and fine with me. After all it was just a summer romance, and I was on my high horse with my friends about how stupid it was for the guys to drink so much beer.

I found out later that Jack wrote the letter for him, or helped him write it. Honest to Pete!

That fall I received a letter from Jack, inviting me to Yale for a football game in New Haven, Connecticut. It was on the same weekend that a ten-year-old camper named Lee, had invited me to New Haven for her birthday. Lee was a dear little girl who looked up to me, the older counselor. Of course I would want to go to her birthday party, but I had said no to her because I had to be somewhere else. When I received Jack's invitation I changed my mind about going to New Haven, and, luckily, my parents allowed me to spend Saturday night after the game at Lee's house with her family.

We had a wonderful time. I found out later why Jack had invited me to Yale. It seems he and his roommate had been to Lee's house for dinner. Lee's brother was a camper at Timanous. Part of the reason for the invite was to get a guy to invite me up so I could be there for Lee's birthday. After the roast of lamb dinner, Lee brought my picture down and asked who would be willing to invite me to the football game. She passed my picture around. Jack got lamb grease on it and Lee burst into tears. To appease Lee he said, "I will." And that is how I got invited to my first football game and my first date with Jack.

The next time we saw each other was at a Christmas dance. I wore a red tulle formal dress. We kissed for the first time. He slept at my Grandmary's house in Upper Montclair. We invited each other to our spring proms: my senior, his freshman prom. And then I went away to Europe for the summer. My Grandmary treated me to the trip, with other granddaughters of her friends, supervised by a high school teacher they knew. Grandmary, a world traveler herself, wanted me to go, partly because I would not have a summer free for at least the next four years in the nursing program at Skidmore College in Saratoga Springs, New York. While I was gone, Jack dated my counselor friends at Camp Wohelo! He wrote letters to me but I didn't get them until I returned home to New Jersey, just before leaving for college. They were all forwarded from various places in Europe. He had missed the crucial lead time you need to send a letter to someone traveling abroad.

COLLEGE

Freshman Year

During my first week of college, I went to the rectory of the Catholic Church in town. I asked the pastor if he would teach me some things about the Catholic faith. He said yes and I think we met every week or two throughout the year, for half an hour or so. It was a bit scary going behind my father's back, but at least I was away from home and wasn't dividing my family over it. I was able to talk things over with Jack, my Catholic boyfriend, who I was becoming fonder of each day. Part of what I loved about him was his Catholic faith, which he knew a lot about.

I began my studies at Skidmore very intently. I studied all the time because the courses were so difficult. Most of them were sciences and a few liberal arts requirements. I took two semesters of anatomy and physiology, two of chemistry, two of English, two of American Government (required by New York State), one semester of microbiology, one of psychology, one of sociology and a great elective semester on Shakespeare. There were papers and exams all the time.

Jack managed to get up to Skidmore a few times that fall. Just before Thanksgiving, he came to visit for a weekend, but I felt sick and went to lie down in my dorm. While I was trying to get my act together, some really strange thoughts swam through my head. *"This guy is really special. I really like him. I feel different. Oh my goodness, I think I have really fallen for him. Is this what being in love is like? It sure is different from how I've felt before. What do I do now? I'm so excited. Shall I tell him? Oh gosh. This is incredible. I'd better get up. I can't stay here in bed knowing I feel like this. I can't sleep. Oh God, what does this mean?"*

When Jack returned for supper I think I could not contain myself. I don't know what I said but something that let him know how special he was to me.

I spent Thanksgiving in the college infirmary with viral pneumonia. I didn't get to go home for the holidays. It was awful. My one consolation was a good book: 'The Cain Mutiny.' Captain Queeg rolling the little balls in his hands and the great adventure of the story helped me ward off my loneliness.

Jack and I continued to date. The college curfew rules in those days were strict. I received my share of demerits for being a few minutes late. I was campused a few times. More time to study, I told myself. Aside from dating, I only had time to go to one movie my freshman year...'Three Coins in The Fountain.' I never cut a class. It wasn't allowed.

NURSING PROGRAM IN NYC, 1955

First Summer

After one year on campus in Saratoga Springs, New York, my college nursing program sent me to New York City. Our home base hospital was New York Post Graduate Hospital, Bellevue Medical Center. It was not the big Bellevue Hospital, but a private hospital associated with it.

In June, 1955, after a brief week's vacation, I moved my stuff into the nurses' residence at 116 East 20th Street, New York City, across the street from the hospital, where the guts of our nursing program began.

That summer was tough. We learned to make beds that quarters could be bounced off of, and how to take vital signs, actually getting correct pulses and blood pressures. We got up at 6:00 a.m., dressed in a starched white uniform with a white apron and a starched white organdy cap, and freshly polished white shoes. We ate breakfast in the cafeteria and arrived on the hospital floor promptly at 7:00 a.m., awake, bright-eyed and bushy tailed, to learn how to care for sick patients. It was hot. Air conditioning was rare in those days, but since running around kept a breeze on our sweaty skin, in a way it felt cool. When I thought about how hot it was for the patients in bed, I didn't feel so hot.

Jack was in Maine working at the camp and I missed him. My Father, who worked in New York City, stayed in our house in New Jersey during the week and went to Rhode Island on weekends. He made the summer festive for me. Daddy took me out for dinner once a week and to a movie or a Broadway play. The best play we saw was 'My Fair Lady.' The worst movie we saw was 'The Man With The Golden Arm' which depressed me terribly. It was about drug addiction but too much like the suffering and sorrow in the hospital.

FALL AND WINTER

The summer ended and Jack was back at Yale. That fall and winter I babysat a lot at Stuyvesant Town and Peter Cooper Village on the lower East Side to earn train fare to New Haven where there were fun things to do and great people to meet. I went a lot. It was my college social life. I needed to be with people my age who were doing things people my age did. Working in a hospital with people of different ages, I learned a lot about life in a hurry. Often I was in over my head. At times I questioned if I belonged there. It was hard. In some respects I was like a fish out of water in nursing. In other respects, I knew I was where I belonged. My mother's early death introduced me to the world of suffering and I had grown accustomed to it.

I wanted to be in an environment where others suffered, where I could help and we could connect. This was a kind of wisdom, and a part of the vocation to nursing that brought me satisfaction.

That year (1955-56) we worked part-time and attended classes part-time at the hospital across the street from the nursing residence. We studied nursing basics, medical and surgical nursing, and pediatrics. After that we affiliated, or studied, for about three months at each of the following hospitals: Cornell Hospital on east 58th Street for Obstetrics and Gynecology, Presbyterian Hospital's Psychiatric Institute on West 168th Street for psychiatric nursing, and the brand new Veteran's Hospital on the East Side, for Veteran's Medicine. We also spent time in many clinics throughout the city. Our total nursing/college program lasted four years and four summers straight through, ending with Public Health Nursing the summer after graduation from college.

BECOMING A ROMAN CATHOLIC

The day I moved into the nurses residence on 20th Street, a letter from Father John F. Donovan, MM (Maryknoll Missionaries) was waiting for me in my mailbox, explaining that my Mother had mentioned I was looking for a priest for instruction in the Catholic faith, and he would be happy to see me if I was interested.

It seems two Maryknoll priests had visited my parents' house in New Jersey to thank my mother for donating money to their order. My next youngest sister would not let them in the door, as instructed, because two robbers in our town had dressed up as a nun and a priest, tied up the owner of a house, put her in a closet and robbed her. Just in the nick of time my mother heard my sister saying, "I can't let you in." My mom opened the door and invited them in for a visit.

During their thank-you visit she told them I'd be in New York City, asked if someone could help me with instructions, and gave them my address.

I called Father Donovan and we began instructions, weekly or bi-weekly, (I can't remember), for more than a year. When I finally decided I did want to become a Catholic, I told my Dad but he was not pleased. He gave me a book to read called, *Why I became a Protestant,* and asked me to talk with our minister. I did both but this did not change my mind.

Arrangements were made and I was baptized in a Catholic parish in Chinatown, New York, on September 22, 1956. It was in Chinatown because Father Donovan had been a missionary for many years in China and this was the church to which he had access. My oldest sister, Cesca, was my godmother and Jack was my godfather. We had a nice Chinese lunch, then went to Immaculate Conception parish in Montclair, where I made my first confession. The next morning we went to the Convent of the Sacred Heart chapel at 91st Street, New York City, where Father Donovan said Mass and I received my first Holy Communion.

My Dad attended this Mass and the beautiful breakfast the good Sacred Heart Sisters gave us afterwards. They even had Cuban cigars for the men! Father Donovan frequently played tennis with the nuns, so they knew each other. They gave me a beautiful holy picture of Mary holding baby Jesus, called the Madonna of the Streets.

Later that year I was confirmed in the Roman Catholic parish church on Second Avenue near the hospital and nurses' residence where I regularly went to Holy Mass.

ENGAGED TO BE MARRIED

I spent many weekends at Yale, dating Jack, and staying with Lee's family. Gradually our love grew deeper. On December 21, 1956 in the lobby of the Psychiatric Institute of Presbyterian Hospital where I was doing my psychiatric affiliation, Jack gave me a special Christmas present...he asked me to marry him and gave me a diamond ring! We had talked about marriage. We both wanted to marry each other. We knew this was it. Without two nickels to rub together, we were determined to make it, somehow.

Jack graduated from Yale in 1957 and began Yale Law School that

New York City and returned to the Skidmore College cam-
aratoga Springs, New York, for my senior year to finish my
nursing degree. Since I had completed most of my nursing courses by
then, I spent the year taking liberal arts courses to round out my education. Jack lent me his car and it became "The Taxi" to New Haven
most week-ends. It was fun being a college girl again. I charged my pas-
sengers $ 5.00 each. It paid for gas. I had one accident. Jack's parents
paid for the radiator I smashed in, skidding on a patch of ice in Great
Barrington, Massachusetts.

MARRIAGE

We made wedding plans for June 14, 1958, the week after my graduation from Skidmore with a Bachelor of Science degree in nursing.
The diploma wouldn't be signed until I finished the summer course in
Public Health Nursing. We had a beautiful wedding. My mother and
sisters worked very hard to arrange all the details. Jack and I went to
the Bear Mountain Inn, in New York, for our one-night honeymoon.
The next Monday I began my public health student nursing rotation,
and Jack began his summer job at the New York Trust Company. We
were absolutely in heaven. We were married at last, for sure, for good.
Life in a way had just begun for me.

We lived in an apartment on 14th Street, New York City, which we
sub-let from some medical students Jack knew at Yale. In September,
we had an apartment waiting for us in New Haven and I had a job
lined up as a visiting nurse there. All we had to do was enjoy the summer in New York, work and write thank-you notes for wedding gifts
before we could settle down in New Haven.

My district as a visiting nurse was Greenpoint Williamsburg in
Brooklyn. Every day I took the subway train to that new territory. It
was fascinating to explore a new part of the New York I had grown up
so close to. My hometown of Montclair, New Jersey was thirty minutes
from New York City proper. As a child I had enjoyed the Metropolitan
Opera, theater, shopping for clothes at Best & Company and Macy's,
as well as other outings. Now I was exploring a whole new part of the

five boroughs of New York. I felt like the City was my oyster, and marriage to Jack was bliss.

MARRIED LIFE

NEW HAVEN, CT

That fall we moved to New Haven, Connecticut for Jack's second year at Yale Law School, and my job as a visiting nurse, in New Haven. Our first child, John, was born April 30, 1959 at Grace New Haven Hospital. Between us, Jack and I had several jobs. Jack coached lacrosse at Yale on spring afternoons and was a night guard at the Armstrong Rubber Tire plant. I worked as a private duty nurse two or three evenings, from 3:00 p.m.-10:00 p.m., each week. Jack and baby John would pick me up and take me to Jimmy's at Savin Rock for a hot dog. Then Jack would drop us off at our apartment and drive off to his night watchman job. Together on weekends we were university chaperones! We'd tour the fraternities at 10:00 p.m. to make sure they had chaperones. We split the job with another couple and we took care of each other's babies. We also chaperoned the freshman, junior and senior proms. We were paid good money for those days, $200.00 a semester. Of course, it was fun.

The next year Jack graduated from law school in June, 1960.

PROVIDENCE, R.I.
(THE EARLY YEARS - 1960-1974)

We moved to Providence , Rhode Island, where Jack began his law career, and I cared for our first child, and carried our second child, Tim, who was born January 2, 1961.

When our third son, Terry, was due in November, 1962, it was time to buy our own house. We found a lovely duplex, (side by side house) for $24,000.00, in St. Sebastian's Parish, on the East Side of Providence. A friendly older couple rented the other side of our house sort of permanently and that helped pay our mortgage.

I was involved in the Junior League, as my Mom had been, where I helped run a children's library at the Children's Center, volunteered at R.I. Hospital and did other volunteer jobs. I also got involved in the Childbirth Education Association (C.E.A.), the forerunner of birthing classes. This enabled husbands to coach their wives through labor and delivery in the hospital. In those days husbands could coach their wives in private labor rooms at Cornell Hospital in New York, and Grace New Haven Hospital in Connecticut, but NOT in Providence, Rhode Island. C.E.A. helped make this possible. When our fourth child was almost due, I, a CEA RN, coached a couple during labor. This was the only way they could be together during labor in the hospital. Then I retired in 1964 to have my own baby girl, Mary.

Jack and I became busier and busier raising our family which grew to six, with the births of a boy named Michael in 1965 and a girl named Joan in 1968.

C.C.D.

Having been raised by parents and taught by schools that it was important to give back to the community, Jack and I volunteered to teach high school Confraternity of Christian Doctrine class one evening a week. I continued with Junior League volunteer work until our parish school suddenly lost its religious sisters and the high school CCD Program fell into my lap.

Joan Rothman, a good friend, took on developing and running the elementary program and I assumed responsibility for the high school program. It was all a learning experience for me. I flew by the seat of my pants and on the wings of the Holy Spirit. As a convert to Catholicism, I was learning so much that I hungered for. I spent hours at the Diocesan Office of Religious Education and on the phone, asking questions and getting good advice on what to do and what to read.

A nun from the Congregation of Notre Dame, Sister Pauline Lindquist, who had worked in our parish, helped me focus and set the stage for the program. She said, "Begin with John 1: 35-39 in the New Testament, where John the Baptist was with two of his disciples."

"The next day John was there again with two of his disciples. As he watched Jesus walk by he said, 'Look! There is the Lamb of God!' The two disciples heard what he said and followed Jesus. When Jesus turned around and noticed them following him, he asked them, 'What are you looking for?' They said to him, 'Rabbi (which means teacher), where do you stay?' 'Come and see,' he answered. So they went to see where he was lodged, and stayed with him that day. (It was about four in the afternoon.)" (John 1:35-39)

We were to point to Jesus and help people look for Him through the Gospels, then stay with Him and really get to know Him. Despite the fact that there were some who were more qualified than I was, I accepted the challenge. It was a very enriching experience.

Pre-Cana / Marriage Preparation

At some point our assistant pastor at St. Sebastian's asked us and another couple, our friends, Barbara and Tony, to teach his senior C.C.D. class about marriage. Then he recruited the four of us to become a Pre-Cana, or marriage prep team, for the Diocese.

Developing ourselves as a team was very hard. We began with a packet of questions about our own marriages and together had to answer them out loud. Things came up regarding Jack's and my relationship that I had never thought about. And there we were, out front and openly looking at ourselves first, before talking to engaged couples.

We met many times, worked up our talks and went on the road to a Brown University Newman Club engaged couples group, sharing with them our living out of the Sacrament of Matrimony. We drew on Church teaching and our own experiences. We explored the practical aspects of marriage, including finances. We were supposed to be helping engaged couples. In fact, they helped us in all the preparation we had to go through.

Barbara, Tony and Jack and I became fast friends and are to this day. Barbara and Tony organized married couple's retreats for us and three other couples who were close friends of theirs. Once a year we'd go off for the weekend to be led by a wonderful Jesuit priest from Boston College, a therapist friend of theirs named Father Jack McCall. The conferences/meditations were so helpful that we kept up those retreats for several years. Fr. McCall led us in a powerful prayerful exercise I remember to this day. It was a meditation on letting go of our own trapeze up in the big tent of life, and grabbing onto God's trapeze, actually deciding to do that in prayer using our imaginations. This made all the difference in my life.

PRAYER MEETINGS

One day in 1970 or 1971, our baby-sitter, also from a large family, said: "You've got to come to a prayer meeting. It's fantastic! We've started going to prayer meetings at Holy Ghost Church. You can talk to my Mom about it. You'd love it."

We went to our first prayer meeting and it was beautiful. First we went to Holy Mass at 7:00 p.m. up in the church, then we went downstairs for the prayer meeting. There were many people seated in concentric circles. They sang Christian songs spontaneously, read Scripture passages out loud, and gave witnesses about Jesus' action in their lives. There was also a teaching given about our Lord Jesus Christ, true God and true man, God the Father and the Holy Spirit, the Holy Scriptures and how to let Jesus become Lord of our lives. Though spontaneous, it was all orderly and synchronized by the Holy Spirit, who inspired these various outpourings of love for God.

People's love for Jesus was very, very beautiful. We took a class called *Life in the Spirit Seminars.* It met after the prayer meetings, for a number of weeks.

I wanted the fullness of this gift of the Holy Spirit, so I read a lot about it, including Henry James' *Varieties of Religious Experience,* which my husband recommended. Then one night when everyone in our house was fast asleep I began to pray: "Lord, if this gift of the Holy Spirit is from you, I believe you will give it to me here in my home, next to my sleeping husband, surrounded by my children sleeping in their beds...in the midst of my family whom I love and take care of for you."

The Lord was very generous as I continued to pray: "I surrender my soul to you, Lord Jesus. Come Lord Jesus, Come into my heart. Come, Holy Spirit, come fill the hearts of your faithful and enkindle in us the fire of your love. Send forth Your Spirit and we shall be created and you shall renew the face of the earth."

I began to experience a great peace and in my mind's eye I saw Jack and me at the altar on our wedding day. Then I saw six little explosions like bright stars where I saw each of our six children born. "I have created you in an explosion of love," I heard God say to me, deep in my heart, and I began to praise God over and over.

That moment was the happiest of my whole life. Praise the Lord!

St. Patrick's Parish
1971-1980

In 1971, Fr. John Randall, the priest who headed the prayer community, and Fr. Raymond Kelly, the librarian at the Diocesan Seminary, received permission from the bishop to move the prayer community to St. Patrick's Parish, in the inner city of Providence, on Smith Hill. It was an experiment to see if the Catholic Charismatic Renewal could actually renew a dying inner city parish that had been cut in half by Interstate 95. Father Raymond Kelly became Pastor of St. Patrick's Parish, and Father Randall continued to lead the prayer group.

By this time many of us had made serious commitments to the prayer community which became known as "The Word of God Community." We tried to base our lives on God's Word in the Holy Scriptures and prayer. Many of us even moved our families into the neighborhood.

This was a prayer community, so actions and decisions were prayed about, and people were growing in great devotion to following God's will in their lives.

Hundreds of people from all over the United States and the world came to visit the parish and attend the prayer meetings. We had ongoing Catholic education. A book table sold many classic Catholic books for spiritual reading, and *Life In The Spirit Seminars* were always being offered.

The community settled into the beautiful, Gothic style St. Patrick's Church, on State Street. But after a couple of years the Diocese of Providence Building Commission declared it unsafe because rain water and snow started seeping in-between the outside and inner walls. "Too much singing and the walls might come tumbling down," someone said.

In the meantime, the community was in the process of reopening the parish school. That building became both our parish church and our school. People with many different talents in the community volunteered to re-furbish the school building and plans were made for a new program from kindergarten to eighth grade. Several excellent teachers chose to staff the school and some recent college graduates began their teaching careers there.

When St. Patrick's Word of God School, as it was known, opened in the fall of 1972, our children were at various stages of schooling. John, our oldest, was to enter eighth grade at St. Sebastian's parish school. He had attended it since kindergarten. Our other children had been moved in and out of St. Sebastian's as elementary grades were lopped off. The departure of the nuns who had taught there, and the financial drain on the parish paying lay teacher salaries, resulted in this unstable situation. A new public elementary school that some of them attended during this crunch time, was also in flux. First they had a third grade; then they took it away for a year. So our son, Terry, had to go to a different school after having been there in second grade. Consequently, he went to three different schools in four years. By now St. Sebastian's school was in the process of being closed. So when St. Patrick's re-opened it seemed the best solution for our children to attend--all but John, whose eighth year was the last time eighth grade was offered at St. Sebastian's School.

Our children came to St. Patrick's school the year it opened. A year later we moved into the parish to be fully a part of what was going on there. We bought a three-story tenement, put in central heat, new electrical wiring, and remodeled it as a one-family house. Moving was a big decision. We waited until all our children said O.K. Many other families from the prayer community did the same. We all hoped that we would be a force for renewing the neighborhood.

The night we moved in and slept in our own beds, there was a raging storm. The house shook. I prayed: "Lord, if it is your will, please calm this storm so my children won't be terrified."

Very soon, the storm subsided. Thank you, God!

The next several years were quite an adjustment for our family and everyone else's family. We were trying our best to do God's will in an inner-city environment. Some teachers in the school lived with us and were paid a very small stipend. Jack and I worked very hard, as did just about everyone, to help St. Patrick's grow. It was very challenging for us and even more so for our children.

Two wonderful elderly, Irish, widowed sisters named Helen and Rita lived next door to us. They babysat for their grand- and great-grandchildren and they helped our family by watching out for us and praying for us. They were the best neighbors we could have had. We moved out of the neighborhood just after Helen and Rita died. I might add that I have met many people who grew up in St. Patrick's in the old days, and they are some of the finest people I know.

The good and the bad of our years at St. Patrick's are all in God's hands now. They were not perfect years but our family learned some very important lessons there. And the Lord did protect us from many things.

A new generation is running things now and the school is prospering, having won many awards for excellence throughout the years.

During those busy years filled with parish commitments, we also spent endless hours watching our children perform in plays and on the athletic fields and ice rinks of Rhode Island, Canada, and much of the rest of the Northeast. As they moved on to college, most of our weekends were spent traveling to visit them, or again, to watch their plays and games.

UNFINISHED BUSINESS - ABOUT MOM

FREE TO BE ME

When my oldest child was in high school, I started dealing with the unfinished business of grieving over my mother's sudden death when I was seven. It had not been safe to grieve or even think about it much at home where I grew up, or after, while I was raising my own six children. I had to survive in both places and keep things together so I could function and take care of every one.

In 1980, one particular event broke through my wall of denial and started me on my way. My husband invited me to an evening of prayer with the St. Patrick's pastoral team of which he was a member. They were reading, discussing and praying through a series of talks by Father John Powell, S.J. called *Free to Be Me*. The series had been on TV.

The topic for the evening was: "*Children are marvelous observers and very poor interpreters.*" We were asked to reflect on our own childhood and look at how this topic might apply to us. We were in prayer. I felt very safe.

Something began bubbling inside of me. When it was my turn to share, I heard myself say: "My mother died suddenly when I was seven while she and I were getting dressed to go to church. She was going to hear me sing in the Christmas children's choir. Right before my eyes she fell to the floor, and died a little time later. When we went to my grandparents' house, somehow I got the idea that I'd caused my mother's death. I *observed* that though she was sick with lumbago in her back, she got out of bed to hear me sing. I heard someone say I wore my mother out. I *interpreted* this all to mean that it was my fault she died."

To my knowledge I never thought or said this before in my life, but it felt as familiar and natural to me as breathing. I felt peaceful and very close to God. I sat still for a long time resting in the arms of God and my new life.

When I returned home from this sharing group I thought about what I had said, and I felt free, free to be me! But I didn't know this guilt for Mom's death lived in me until I heard myself say it. Our bed was piled high with clean unfolded laundry. With great ease and joy, I folded all those clothes and went to bed very happy.

Early the next morning I had the most amazing dream—it seemed like a real experience. I dreamed my Mom and I were in a cabin in Vermont, just the two of us. We sat on the bed and chatted away, catching up on life. I told her all about her wonderful grandchildren, my children. Just being together was so great. It seemed so natural, gabbing away as we would if she were still alive. In fact, I sensed in God's Providence that we had been together for a moment. I woke up feeling a new completeness.

FUNERAL OF MICHELLE'S MOTHER

Some time later, following this period of peace, I went to the funeral of the mother of one of the kindergarteners in our school. I cried for little Michelle. And I cried for myself. I had to admit the truth. I cried for that little child in me who had to stop crying when my father married again and brought a new mother and three new sisters into our family. My baby sister, brother, and I had to welcome them. They came to live in our house in our town. Our lives changed dramatically. I felt somewhat displaced even though they were my summertime friends and very good people.

Years of suppressed pain started welling up inside of me as I sobbed after Michelle's mother's funeral. Once the floodgates opened, I couldn't turn back. I couldn't take back my secret suppressed life and truck along like business as usual. I never realized until then what I had hidden there. Emotions and thoughts I had hidden down deep began surfacing. It was like an avalanche. Some of it felt good. Some of it was very frightening.

I crashed and isolated myself. I read a lot and prayed a lot. Through my isolation I had a sense that I was on to something big and important, even lifesaving. I felt my life was at stake, and I'd better fight for it now or I would perish. It was my life this time and not everyone else's. This was a strange place for me because I was used to forgetting or hiding myself and putting others first.

This change of course was unsettling for my family. I couldn't respond to their needs as I had before. I felt angry and resentful. I had tried so hard not to "wear anyone out" that I wore myself out! My frustrations led me to act in ways that were unlike me. I became a person I couldn't recognize. I didn't know how to handle my feelings. I couldn't explain to my family what was going on because I didn't know myself. I needed the space to work out these things which I couldn't explain then but now know were delayed grief and post-traumatic stress reactions.

And so I went for therapy to a counselor a priest had recommended. And I went for spiritual direction to a very holy Catholic Sister, named Kieran Flynn, RSM, who ran a retreat house in the country by the sea. I took my counseling issues to Sister and she helped me pray through them. Sister taught me how to bring them to God in prayer. For example, she might say, "Pray this passage in the Bible, stay with it all day." Or, "Take a resurrection walk. Look for signs of resurrection in nature." In addition to seeing Sister Kieran monthly, I went on several silent, directed weekend retreats during the eighties. The grounds of the retreat house were beautiful and therapeutic, near the ocean and nestled in a mini-forest. Jesus was there in those peaceful surroundings and at the retreat house in the Blessed Sacrament all day and all night. I could pour out my heart to Him and receive as much of His help as I wanted.

CHAPTER II

HOMEWARD BOUND - DAD
CHRISTMAS, 1980

My Dad was diagnosed with colon cancer in the spring of 1980. He took part in a trial for Laetril, an experimental cancer fighting drug, at Sloan Kettering Hospital in New York City. I do not know if he had a placebo or the real thing, but we hoped for the best, even though he developed another tumor in his groin.

After Thanksgiving I went on an eight-day silent retreat that I had been preparing for in prayer. It was time for me to be apart, be reconciled with my mother's death, repent and be healed of some darkness in my soul. I went to the beautiful retreat house near the ocean, where I had my own room, good food to eat, two chapels with the Blessed Sacrament present for prayer, daily Holy Mass, a spiritual director to see a short while each day, great woods, ocean paths, silence and solitude, time alone with God and His creation. There were other people on retreat there. Our gift to each other was silence, solitude, and prayer.

One subject of my prayer was my Dad. I prayed the Seven Last Words of Christ using a book by Matthew and Dennis Lynn, called *Healing The Dying*. I used the meditations on the last words of Christ and prayed for my Dad and me. In the chapel and in my room, I wrote letters to Dad, and listened to what he might say to me in return, and wrote it down. I would bring all this to God in the presence of the Blessed Sacrament in the chapel. We'd talk it all over and I would listen to what God had to say. I discovered Daddy as my human father and God as my Eternal Father. Both were loving and quite different.

When I arrived home I called to see how my father was doing. He had fallen and was now bedridden. Since I had no idea how long he would be alive, I wanted to see him. He said to me on the phone: "Don't come just to see me, come to help your mother out." My husband and children were wonderful and agreed I should go the next day.

During this time I had been rehearsing the part of Elizabeth, cousin of the Virgin Mary, Mother of Christ, for a Christmas nativity play in my parish. My part began with "The Visitation", when Mary visited her cousin, Elizabeth, who was pregnant with John the Baptist, after the Angel Gabriel announced to Mary she had conceived Jesus by the Holy Spirit.

My short lines became my Advent prayer, as I rehearsed them to myself over and over again. They were: "*How is it that the mother of my Lord would honor me with a visit? The moment I heard your greeting, the babe in my womb leapt for joy,*" referring to John the Baptist. I thought many times of one of my other lines: "*He will turn the hearts of fathers towards their children.*"

My Dad became weaker and ate less each day. Mom made him vegetable drinks in the blender and he was able to eat and enjoy special Comice pears from, I believe, Harry and David's catalogue, sent by Aunt Mary, his sister. Not knowing how long he would need full care, or how long he would live, we hired a night nurse so we could sleep.

My nativity play was to be performed on two nights the week before Christmas. I had an understudy. I missed my family, the house, and Christmas preparations. We always made batches of sinfully delicious Heath-bar-like crunch candy to give as gifts. So I asked Daddy if I should go back to do the play and see my family. I wanted him to call the shots for me one more time. "Yes, go do the play, see your family and then come back," he said.

I went home for the Thursday evening dress rehearsal, and asked the cast to pray for my father and my family. It seemed so incredible that I had arrived at that point in my adult life when my father, my other parent, was dying and taking time to do so. I felt normal in a sense. This is how many parents die," I thought. "They get sick and in time, their bodies just give out." This time I wanted to take advantage of going through the whole process of Dad's journey to God because Mom had died so fast. My husband knew this. My children pitched in so I could. They all came to the play Friday night then the next day they piled in the car and drove to New Jersey to visit Grandpa and, in their own way, to say good-bye. They returned home that night.

I stayed and took part in the play Saturday night. Then on Sunday I said goodbye to my family once again, and drove back to New Jersey to relieve my sister, Heather. We decided that she should go home for Christmas Day to be with her children, since they were so young. Heather and I had experience in caring for the dying. But my brother, Bruce, and stepmother were also terrific caregivers. Bruce stopped by often because he lived and worked in town.

My nephew, Michael, a medical student, came for a few days to help. He knew how to listen and converse with a dying person, thank heavens, because one of Dad's last three conversations went like this. Sleepily, Dad said: "Calculator." My nephew replied, "Your calculator?" Dad said, "Yes." Nephew: "What do you want with your calculator?" Dad: "Measure." Dad was a civil engineer. "Decision, did I do the right thing? Medicine, Laetril did I do all I could?" I replied, "Yes, Daddy," I replied, "you did everything you could." We were so thrilled to make the connection. Then he slipped back into his semi-comatose sleep.

When he awoke we were alone. I asked him if he wanted to pray. "Yes," he said. "What is your favorite prayer?" I asked. "Create in me a clean heart, O God," he replied. Together we continued praying Psalm 51, "...and renew a right spirit within me. Cast me not away from your presence and take not thy Holy Spirit from me. Restore unto me the joy of your salvation, and uphold me with a willing spirit." Daddy went to sleep again and I was at peace.

The last thing I clearly heard my dad say was, "Alarm, burglars. Mother, alarm." "Yes, Dad. Do you want Mom to have an alarm system?" "Yes," he replied.

"We will make sure she gets an alarm system," we assured him.

On Christmas Eve, Mom and I ate supper next to Daddy's bed. He slept most of the time. Music filled the cold, crisp, clear night air. Christmas carolers sang on our front lawn under Daddy's window. How beautiful, how serene and joyful that night was.

Mom and I exchanged a small Christmas gift with one another: a scarf, a piece of jewelry. I don't remember. Our biggest gift was that serene and peaceful watch that we were sharing together.

The night nurse arrived and we went to bed, while Daddy continued his deep sleep.

Christmas Day came and went. A kind soul came to be with Daddy, so Mom and I could go to Christmas Mass together. We talked about whether Dad should be cremated or buried when he died. It would be a Protestant funeral, not a wake and Catholic Holy Mass. I did not want him cremated because I've always liked reverencing the person's body as Catholics do, but I made it clear it was her choice. "You'll know what to do. You'll just know when the time comes," I said.

My sister returned. I phoned my family to say it could be any time now. *"Grandpa's in a deep coma. He's not talking any more."* My brother returned and together we bathed Dad, changed him, shaved him, and rubbed his back. We all took turns by his side for that day.

The night nurse came at 10:00 p.m. and we kissed Daddy goodnight. Each of us went to our separate rooms.

Sometime earlier I had asked God, if it was His will, to let me be with my father at the moment of his death. I was willing not to be there, but I really wanted to be there. Out of a deep sleep at 1:00 a.m., on December 27, I woke up with a start, threw on my bathrobe, and with my sister who heard me, ran to Daddy's room. His time had come. His breathing was different. It was labored. We rushed to either side of him, held his hands and each whispered, "We love you, Daddy. We are here."

He gasped and woke up with a start, opened his eyes wide and looked at each of us, bright eyed, as if to say goodbye. "Into your hands O Lord I commend his spirit," I silently prayed, as my Dad relaxed, closed his eyes and took his last breath.

Now the day is over
Night is drawing nigh
Shadows of the evening
Peel across the sky.

Mom and my brother arrived at some point.

We called the doctor to come and he "pronounced" my father's death. We waited for the undertaker, wrapped in our own reflections, adoring this man who meant so much to each of us, adoring the precious body we had so lovingly cared for, bathed, fed and comforted as best we could in his discomfort. I felt the sacred journey of his soul going to meet God and the holy angels accompanying him on his way. It was a time to ask his forgiveness, to forgive, and to pray for his soul.

The undertaker came and put Daddy's body in a black body bag. "He will not be cremated," Mother said. She had made her decision. I was thrilled. We could continue to reverence his body at the funeral and see it beforehand if we wanted to. He wouldn't just be ashes in an urn as my mother had been. He will be buried in the ground, in the tradition of my adopted Catholic faith.

We had a lovely funeral. His children all read Scriptures, some said a few words and my brother gave a eulogy. I read Psalm 51.

We had a large luncheon back at the house for relatives and friends, then I returned to Providence with my family. My other sisters stayed with Mom for some days before returning to their homes.

HARVARD HEARS A MOTHER'S PLEA

JUNE 10, 1982

Excitement fills the air! Today is the day we've been waiting ages to see. This morning our first child, John, will become a graduate of Harvard University, with honors.

We park the car and walk to Harvard Yard to find our graduate and his roommates somewhere in the huge crowd that seems like "ten thousand men and women of Harvard" in their black academic robes. Some wear arm bands protesting Apartheid. Banners protesting other things weave through the crowd.

"There's John over there by that tree," says Tim, John's brother, who studies here also. With hugs and kisses we greet and, after a brief visit, leave to find our seats.

We take our seats in the warm spring sun. Gentle breezes promise we won't swelter. The university band plays wonderful classical and pop music. I settle down, take off my shoes and look around.

There are distinguished-looking people everywhere. Some are reading newspapers. "There must be interesting conversations going on all around us," I muse, too busy to listen in just now. The stage is what fascinates me. It seems miles away, covered with a huge striped canopy flying festive flags. I dream about what will be happening there soon. John will receive his degree and Mother Teresa of Calcutta, a living saint, will be there too, most likely praying for us all.

I settle in, collect myself, and reminisce. Memories flood my mind in single file and clusters, beginning with my childhood! My Mother's sudden death, followed by two difficult years. Then my father's remarriage, bringing me a blended family of a new mother and her three daughters, my summer friends who then became my sisters, summers at the beach and camp, high school, college, engagement to Jack, my graduation as a nurse, our wedding, my husband's law studies, my work as a visiting nurse, and John's birth. Then five more wonderful children, a million diapers, a billion meals, car pools, errands, entertaining friends, squabbles, giggles, broken bones. First Confessions,

First Communions, Mass on Sunday, Confirmations, driving lessons, phone calls home. Sports practices and games by the hundreds – hockey, lacrosse, soccer, football, wrestling, golf, sailing, dramatic plays and musicals. Sacrifices made each day. Disasters, victories all at once, and love that bound us through all this. There was homework, there were tests, and college applications. Jobs and money, and tuition, laced with hefty expectations.

John had left in 1976 for two years of prep school at Phillips Exeter Academy and then for Harvard.

"Has it only been twenty-three years since John was born?", I wonder, as I sit preparing to see him graduate. "So much has happened in such a short span of time."

Next week we'll say good-bye again. John will leave first for Europe for a month, then to Kingston, Jamaica, for two years to teach poor high school boys at St. George's College. We have another missionary in the family – a Jesuit International Volunteer. He wants to give before he settles down. I'm proud of him but I'll miss him so.

What's this? I am distracted by students passing newspapers down our row – The Harvard Crimson, The Harvard Gazette, The Boston Globe, all with headlines of Mother Teresa of Calcutta's Class Day speech the previous day, and her picture. I wrap up my memories, smile to myself and think, "Life has been very good to me," and I thank the Lord for taking such good care of us.

My heart pounds as I read the Boston Globe. We missed Mother Teresa's Class Day speech the day before to attend the high school graduation of John's sister, Mary. Now I can read Mother Teresa's words. In a way, I didn't miss it after all. Quoting from the Boston Globe:

"In a highly unusual address (to students yesterday), Mother Teresa, the 'angel' of Calcutta issued a personal call to Jesus and a return to family life marked by chastity, love, prayer, sharing of material wealth and reverence for unborn life.

"Presented to an exuberant audience of more than 3,000 people as a point of reconciliation within different religious beliefs, the tiny missionary, a winner of the Nobel Peace Prize, caused a hush to come over the crowd as she told them:

'You and I have been called here to love one another. To be kind to one another. Let us preach not by words but by example.
Go in search of the poor. If you find them, you will love them. And if you love them, you will serve them.

I do not want people (merely) to share their abundance. I want them to give until it hurts.'

While waiting for her turn at the podium, she sat with her head bowed, silently saying the rosary. The solemnity of her speech and manner stood in absolute contrast to the light-hearted tradition of the day....."

'If a mistake is made' she said, referring to unintended pregnancy, 'have the courage to accept the child. The greatest sin is to destroy the child, the creation of God.'....

"She said many of the same things at Harvard that she has said elsewhere in the world, including at the acceptance of the Nobel Prize for Peace in 1979: Abortion is the greatest evil of all. If a mother can kill her own child, then what hope is there for the rest of us?

'Greater than physical hunger in the world,' she said, 'here is a terrible hunger for love, a terrible hunger for the word of God.'

The ceremonies begin with the great procession of soon to-be graduates and honorary degree recipients.

Hanging on every word of Mother Teresa's in the Boston Globe, I suddenly hear a man's voice coming from way down front: "Mr. President," the Dean proclaims, "I present to you candidates for the degree of Bachelor of Arts." In a powerful booming voice, President Derek Bok replies: "By the power vested in me, I confer on these candidates the degree of Bachelor of Arts and welcome them into the community of educated men and women." After all undergraduate and graduate degrees are presented, it is time for the honorary degrees.

President Bok then calls out Mother Teresa's name. She gets up and walks over to the president. "Mother Theresa," he announces, reading her citation, "her faith, her love, her indomitable will have set an example of compassionate generosity that awakens the conscience of the world."

I am lost in thought, inspired, I feel secure. A part of me, my inside life, feels less alone. My soul feels safe, wrapped in a mother's loving truth. It feels so good to have such peace. I whisper to myself: "Thank you, Jesus, for your presence here."

Gradually during the ceremonies, the peace and grace of the moment express themselves in little glimmers. I remember my mother's last words to me as she lay on her bedroom floor dying, **"No dear, I'm not going to die."** It seems like she is with us here today.

And then a voice inside my inner self reminds me that the suffering that resulted from my mother's sudden death has made me strong and helped me through my life. Today I know I do not suffer alone. I'm not the only one who has borne such weight. Today I know that others suffer too. Women who have had abortions suffer this same deep sense of loss and I believe some are in this crowd today.

Is this a prophet's dream, a hunch of something yet to come, I ask myself. The love I now feel for those who have had abortions must be from God himself, I think. Our mutual silent grief makes part of me feel more complete. Our shared pain has brought me out of an interior isolation.

I am pulled back to the here and now as the assembly sings the Harvard hymn. Someone gives benediction. The "meeting" is adjourned. A ground swell of whoops and hollers and popping champagne corks mix with great applause. The university band strikes up festive music. As the awesome academic procession marches out, we locate John. We rush as calmly as we can to congratulate our son.

THREADS OF MERCY

My son graduated on this day and, in a sense, I did too. He completed his college degree. I completed my job of helping my first child graduate from college.

But that wasn't all! I knew that day that the trauma of Mom's death, hidden for so long, was transformed by the Holy Spirit. My conscience was awakened. I began to feel compassion for mothers and fathers who have lost their babies through abortion. I understood that their pain mirrored mine. I was the child and they were the parents. We were grieving for our lost ones and feeling guilty.

I felt a deep inexpressible call to love them. In loving them I could love Christ. How, I did not know. Compassion seemed enough that day.

I felt my mother calling me from God's heart to love.

YOU WERE CREATED IN AN EXPLOSION OF LOVE

When does life begin? I needed to get to the bottom of many questions. Answers came in different ways. The following prayer experience answered this question for me: when does life begin?

In September, 1982, I began a three-year course called The Spirituality of Christian Leadership, at Our Lady of Peace Spiritual Life Center, the retreat house in the country by the sea. On the first night of the course, Sister Kieran Flynn R.S.M., led us in the following meditation;

"We will begin with our beginnings, our creation. God created man in the image of Himself, male and female He created them. (cf Genesis 1: 26). We were all created in an explosion of God's love at some point in time. Scripture tells us in Psalm 139:

'It was You who created my inmost self
and put me together in my mother's womb
for all these mysteries I thank you,
for the wonder of myself, for the wonder
of your works......
If I flew to the point of sunrise
Or westward across the sea
Your hand would still be guiding me,
Your right hand holding me.'"

But who am I? If I write down all my titles, all the things that I say I am and total them, I am still more than that. I am much more than this to God.

I belong not just to an earthly family, to my family of origin, my ancestors, but also I belong to the family of God. We possess Biblical son-ship or daughter-ship. God's Kingdom is within us and we are called to know who we are as children of God.

Sin or sinfulness, being the opposite or absence of good,(Catechism of the Catholic Church, glossary, p.878) means that I diminish myself or someone else, by being something less than God created me to be. Less than the holiness He calls me to strive for.

Because we are limited and human, and live in time, we put boundaries around the infinity of God. But there are no boundaries. Each of us can move through these supposed boundaries, to touch God's infinite love more and more through prayer.

As I sat in the little chapel at Our Lady of Peace, praying, I felt secure. "Your arms, Lord, are the real beginnings before I lost my mom, became confused and failed in many ways."

And so it was in this place where God grew me up again. God turned my pain around and transformed it into new life.

POST-ABORTION MARKINGS OF MERCY

During the Spirituality of Christian Leadership Course, the sense that people suffer after abortion grew in me. I worried that someday we could meet a post-abortion crisis. The crisis I saw involved both people who have had abortions and others who have been part of them. I sensed the crisis would hit individually and collectively when the denial of what abortion is wears off. Many of the people who are experiencing trauma have trouble speaking out. Many are shut down, isolated and depressed. They are very busy coping with the stress of having aborted a baby, and have often aborted their hopes and dreams for the future.

In my case, the darkest part of me, believing I would destroy anyone I loved as I believed I had destroyed my Mother by wearing her out, became transformed into the gift of reaching out to people suffering after abortion.

I have to say that throughout this entire discovery I sensed basic truths about grieving a loss. These truths were imbedded in me since the day my Mom died suddenly when I was seven. I had locked them away, guarding them carefully those forty years. Now was my time to unlock the door and take my feelings out, oh so carefully. Through prayer and study I found a safe place to discover and deal with my locked up grief. Nobody knew I was connecting with my own sorrow except me. I now see that it was such a fragile process that it had to be done under cover of a purposeful good deed, an intellectual pursuit of a reality that affected other people: post-abortion suffering. This way I could look at my own grief too. To face it head on could have been so terrifying that I might have closed up, closed the door and walked away from healing and resolving my own grief, guilt, and fear of being abandoned.

I HATE CHRISTIANS

Some more Markings of Mercy came into my life pointing me in the direction of post-abortion suffering. One marking was the words of a doctor who performed abortions.

"I HATE CHRISTIANS.....
BECAUSE THEY KNOW THEY ARE FORGIVEN AND I
KNOW GOD WILL NEVER FORGIVE ME FOR WHAT
I DO."

This was a shocker. It turned out to be the cry of many post-abortion women and men... God will never forgive me for what I did.

That fall of 1982 Jack and I made a weekend retreat together at Our Lady of Peace Spiritual Life Center. We chose to interrupt the quiet prayerful Saturday evening because of friends who meant a great deal to us. They had invited us to be with them and we felt the need to socialize as well as be on retreat. Jack was in the middle of a hard stint at work that kept us very tied up and unavailable to be with friends. We needed a break. It was hard to leave the retreat, but we made the drive from the country back to the city with a key to the retreat house. I don't know what we missed by interrupting our solitude with God, but He blessed our evening out in an odd sort of way.

During the course of the evening a surgeon friend of ours at the party told me something very sad. He talked about an abortion doctor he knew who recently told him: "I hate Christians because they know they are forgiven, and I know God will never forgive me for what I do."

That night, we returned to the silence and solitude of the retreat house, to the peaceful forest-like environment by the sea. But the abortion doctor's remarks haunted me. Up to that time I was not fully aware of how widespread the use of abortion was. His statement shocked and horrified me and I could not shake it.

The next morning when I woke up, I wrote a prayer poem. In the silence and solitude of retreat, I poured my heart out to God. I was angry, hurt, confused, over what I had heard the night before. And I felt helpless. Putting pen to paper, I was able to wade through my thoughts and feelings about what this might mean.

Once I identified my own feelings and feeble understanding of how the doctor's words had affected me, I began to experience great compassion for this man. My God, what a tragic situation he was in, believing that God would never forgive him, or not wanting to believe God could forgive him, or not wanting to give up doing abortions. I started carrying on a silent dialogue with this doctor.

I was now on another journey. If someday he said those very same words to me, or if somebody else did, what would I say? What could I say to offer this man or another hope in forgiveness? What did I know about forgiveness?

In my heart and mind and soul, almost daily I was formulating a response for this doctor, whose name I did not know. His statement gripped me with a tremendous desire to experience, somehow personally, God's forgiveness for abortion. I wanted desperately for him to know that forgiveness was available for all of us sinners. We just had to want it and seek it.

I live in the smallest state in the Union. Many of us meet sooner or later. It was not unrealistic that I might encounter this doctor. I wanted to be able to share with him the good news of God's forgiveness and mercy. I began pulling my thoughts together on my typewriter, preparing for our chance meeting or perhaps a letter to the editor. Some of my thoughts were:

"Now it's not true that God will never forgive the doctor for what he is doing. God loves a repentant sinner, and all heaven rejoices when one sinner repents. If part of what we are dealing with, in the escalation of abortion, is people stuck in an endless cycle with no hope of escape, maybe we can start thinking about God's love for them. Maybe we can start thinking about how we can have Christ's heart and compassion for them. God is rich in mercy and He calls us also to be rich in mercy. If we know that one person feels hopelessly outside of God's mercy, then perhaps we could find ways to show that mercy to him. Those involved in abortion suffer pain and distress. Jesus loves them and came to bring them liberty and freedom too.

Jesus said:

'He (God) has sent me to bring the good news to the poor, to bind up hearts that are broken; to proclaim liberty to captives, freedom to those in prison, to proclaim a year of favor from The Lord.'

Isaiah 61: 1,2; Luke 4:18,19

I know that Jesus:
'Will not argue or shout, or make loud speeches in the streets. He is gentle to those who are weak, and kind to those who are helpless. He will persist until He causes justice to triumph, and on Him all peoples will put their hope.'

Isaiah 42: 2, 3

I believe Jesus has great compassion toward people who perform or have abortions. He knows better than anyone the dilemma they are in. We are all God's children. We have all gone astray in one way or another. Our hope is in the way God loves us."

These were some of my thoughts.

LIKE A CUP OF COFFEE

NOVEMBER, 1982

Soon after the retreat, I learned that my friend, Mary, who was pregnant for the fourth time, went to her HMO for a pregnancy test. She was happily married, struggling gracefully to take care of her young family which included her husband and three dear little boys. We had a lot in common: faith, joys, maternity, babies and hope for the future through our children in whom we invested everything we were and had.

Mary's pregnancy test was positive. When the HMO person told her this news, she asked Mary: "Was this pregnancy planned?"

Mary said: "No," shocked at this intruding question. The health maintenance person then asked Mary, who was in her thirties, if she wanted to have an amniocentesis test to see if her baby was normal. Mary said, "No."

Then, as apparently required by law, like offering Mary a cup of coffee she was asked: "Do you want to terminate this pregnancy?"

Mary bolted from the office to her car where she fell apart, shattered. She felt brutalized. Her sobs ran wild. "I'm pregnant. I want this child, difficult as this may be. Someone asked if this pregnancy was planned, then asked if I wanted amniocentesis because of my age, and then did I want an abortion. My God! I need support. Where is it? How will I ever come back here again for the rest of my pregnancy for check-ups? I know that health person was telling me what she had to legally, but this is insane. I must go home now to the kids and my husband. Help me Lord."

Mary told me about this on the telephone. I was furious at this monstrous betrayal of the sanctuary of the womb. I saw it as an invasion of aliens, alien thoughts, alien actions, and alien evil knocking at the door of my friend's life as well as my own.

At this point I found myself in real trouble. I entered into combat with an anger I had never experienced before. When I studied nursing, my favorite affiliation was maternity nursing. This brought me in contact with the incredible miracle of birth. And I had experienced this miracle first hand, as I carried and gave birth to our six children.

But I found myself raging over the injustice of abortion. How dare they kill an innocent unborn child who depends on his parents and society for nurturing and sustenance while he or she develops in the womb? I groped for hope in God from going crazy myself, as I confronted the horror that people were aborting babies, that innocent mothers were being offered abortions as casually as being offered a cup of coffee, and that one abortion doctor hated Christians because "they know they are forgiven...that God would never forgive me for what I do."

It was horrible to wake up to the fact that, since 1973, abortion had become legal and MILLIONS of babies had died since then. I had much to learn, most of which I wanted nothing to do with. I continued my journey into forgiveness, and the mercy of God, the only way

I knew to get through this. I started calling my effort "Forgiveness for Abortion."

Speaking of anger, Father John Powell, S.J. in his book, *Abortion, the Silent Holocaust,* cautions that "love is the only way to go." And I remembered those very words I heard from Mother Teresa of Calcutta, three months earlier at Harvard Graduation: "You and I have been called here to love one another, to be kind to one another. Let us preach not by words but by example....We can't do for all the poor, so let us begin with one."

A while after my phone call with Mary, I wrote the following letter titled *COURAGE,* to the Editor of The Providence Visitor, our diocesan weekly newspaper. My thoughts for people struggling with pregnancy, which often can be very difficult, were published a few days before Christmas in 1982.

COURAGE

DECEMBER 1982

I wish to encourage all pregnant women who carry new life within them. I want to commend them for their courage to nurture and sustain life in this day and age. A newly pregnant woman is extremely vulnerable. The call within her biologically, psychologically and spiritually draws her to make way for new life. It is an all-encompassing call. She is compelled from the marrow of her bones, to the deepest regions of her soul, to receive and nurture new life. It begins in tiny whispers and builds increasingly each day. It peaks in the crescendo of bringing forth a new child, mysterious and wonderful, to this earth.

I believe there is a master plan in pregnancy, one of growth towards life at any level, that we cannot ignore.

I have been a pregnant woman six times. I am also a registered nurse. I know this call to cooperate with nature. I know some of what it takes to make way for new life developing within me and others. I also know how shaky, frightened and inadequate a newly pregnant woman feels. Our internal life runs the scale from strong fears of inadequacy to heights of joy. We have an outrageous desire to protect this new life. We don't know how we will manage this life-giving process that is beyond us, but we know we must somehow, at all cost. It takes yielding, courage and support to integrate this new experience. There is a rhythm to how it goes. Each step is vital to the life and well-being of the pregnant woman and her child.

My heart was torn last week. It still is. Crude questions, death knelling questions were asked a newly pregnant friend of mine at a Rhode Island health care facility. The person in Ob-Gyn gave my waiting anxious friend the test results of positive pregnancy. After the news was given, my friend was asked, "Was this pregnancy planned?" This is no one's business but the woman and her mate. My vulnerable friend, trying to adjust to the new call on her life, answered honestly, in the face of earth-shattering conceptual news, "No." Then, like being offered a cup of coffee she was asked, "Would you like to have this pregnancy terminated?"

I ask those people who propose such questions: Do you know what you are doing? Do you know yourselves?

Joan C. Pendergast
Providence"

I had to say something. I could not remain silent. It was the best I had to offer at the time.

INTO THE HEART OF A DOOMED LAND

God is a stern warrior of love. I wondered, are we doomed in this land because we abort babies?

In December, 1982, I attended a weekend retreat given by Father George A. Aschenbrenner, S.J., at Our Lady of Peace Spiritual Life Center. The following is from the retreat brochure:

"December 17-19 (1982) George Aschenbrenner, SJ
When peaceful silence lay over all,
and night had run the half of her swift course,
down from the heavens, from the royal throne,
leapt your all-powerful Word;
into the heart of a doomed land
the stern warrior leapt.

Wisdom 18: 14-15
The experience of forgiveness reveals and integrates all our energies for living and for loving as sons and daughters of a loving Father. This Weekend will explicate the interior of this experience of forgiveness."

Here are some of the touchstones from that weekend's note-taking:

"Forgiveness is the birthplace of a
great zeal to serve, to love, to give
myself for others.

From the Ascension through Pentecost,
the Church is born in forgiveness.

We are born in forgiveness for being traitors,
for betraying Christ. We are all sinners,
and we can all be forgiven.
Ministry is born in forgiveness."

This retreat was astounding to me. After reviewing the state of the Sacrament of Reconciliation in the Catholic Church, with all the changes since Vatican Council II, we took a very deep look at what forgiveness means, how Jesus is the Father's forgiveness.

One picture that stands out in my mind is the scene during Jesus' trial, when He was being taken from his session with Pontius Pilate to the balcony where people were to decide whether to release Him or Barabbas. His apostles were isolated from Jesus. They were scattered and trying to save their own necks during this confusing and frightening time. Peter had just denied that he knew Jesus and was scrambling to save his own identity. As Jesus made the trip to the balcony, His eyes found Peter's eyes, after Peter had denied Him three times and the cock had crowed. His gaze was a gaze of love, as if saying, "Peter, Peter, I love you...Oh, Peter, I forgive you for denying that you know me."(Luke 22: v.61).

That gaze of Christ's love melted Peter's heart. That gaze of forgiveness transformed Peter's shame into the security of experiencing that he was loved unconditionally. No strings, just that quick, cleansing piercing gaze of love.

Another picture that stays with me from the retreat is the "woman known in the town to be a sinner," bending over Jesus' feet when he was in Simon's house, bathing his feet with perfumed oil. Simon said to himself, "If this man were a prophet, he would know who and what sort of woman this is that touches him - that she is a sinner."

In answer to his thoughts, Jesus said to him, after proposing a parable on forgiveness: "You see this woman? I came to your home and you provided me with no water for my feet. She has washed my feet with her tears and wiped them with her hair. You gave me no kiss but she has not ceased kissing my feet since I entered. You did not anoint my head with oil, but she has anointed my feet with perfume. I tell you, that is why her many sins are forgiven - because of her great love. Little is forgiven the one whose love is small" (Luke 7: v.37-40, 44-47).

Somewhere at some time this woman had also met the gaze of Jesus' amazing love and it changed her life. Somehow she, too, had experienced his forgiveness and felt His mercy. When she heard He was in town she burst in on the dinner party and rushed to his feet to anoint them and dry them with her hair. It was her way of saying thanks. Jesus knew as He knows things, that she was expressing her gratitude for being set free from her shame. He knew that her great love was a result of her experience of forgiveness.

And then there is the other picture of the woman caught in adultery, in the process of being stoned for her crime. Jesus was there too, doodling in the sand. "Let the one among you who is without sin be the first to throw a stone at her," He said.

The men walked away one by one. After a while, Jesus and the woman were the only ones left. "Has no one condemned you, Jesus asked?"

She replied, "No one, Sir."

Then Jesus said: "Neither do I condemn you. Go, and from now on do not sin any more." (John 8: 1-11)

Here is another act of forgiveness coupled with the truth that she had indeed sinned but didn't have to any more. There was a better way, a life of peace that comes with mercy and forgiveness. For the first time in her life, she experienced true love.

1983: POPE JOHN PAUL II
AND THE HOLY YEAR OF REDEMPTION

As you may remember, on May 13, 1981, during a general audience in St. Peter's Square in Rome, a man named Mehmet Ali Agca, a professional assassin, shot Pope John Paul II at point blank range. "The bullet that struck the Pope missed the main abdominal artery by the merest fraction of an inch. Had the artery been struck, John Paul would have bled to death before being transferred from the Pope-mobile to the ambulance. Moreover, the bullet that might have paralyzed him, missed his spinal column and every major nerve cluster in its potential path." [1] The Pope was rushed to the hospital. It was miraculous that he did not die. "....He attributed his survival to the intercession of the Virgin. John Paul said he believed her hand had diverted the bullet Agca had shot."[2]

"In 2005, John Paul spoke of his assassin in *Memory and Identity*. He said that he had forgiven his assassin even before he knew who he was, even before he arrived at the hospital to be operated on. His forgiveness was among his last thoughts before he lost consciousness." [3]

"After he was shot, after he had forgiven Agca, John Paul found himself pondering whether Agca understood that the man he tried to kill had freely and fully forgiven him. He realized he wanted to tell him this himself. So during Christmas week 1983, the Pope went to the Rebibbia prison in Rome. There he celebrated Mass; then he went to Agca's cell, where they sat together in plastic chairs, just the two of them, and talked."[4] "John Paul met with Mehmet Ali in his prison cell, and spent two hours with him. He listened to him, told him about the Catholic faith, embraced him, and forgave him."[5]

The cover of Time Magazine showed the Holy Father telling Agca he forgave him. It was a powerful picture that influenced me greatly. It made the Holy Father's announcement of the Holy Year of Redemption that December deeply hopeful for me. As I heard and read about the Holy Year, I learned that Christians throughout the world would be praying for reconciliation among people, with God, and each other. The Pope called all Christians, all men and women to a fresh commitment to reconciliation.

As I read and prayed through this beautiful papal document, I was in awe of God's mercy for me in my life and His call to repentance and

1 Weigel, *WITNESS TO HOPE, The Biography of Pope John Paul II*, 413-414.
2 Noonan, *JOHN PAUL THE GREAT: Remembering A Spiritual Father*, 61.
3 Ibid, 59.
4 Ibid, 61.
5 Ibid, 57-58.

reconciliation to all of us. The fact that the Church in the whole world would be praying for this, beginning on March 25, 1983, to Easter Sunday, April 22, 1984, was very exciting to me. I saw it as a huge help for people struggling after abortion – that people throughout the world would be praying for them.

ON THE SCRAP HEAP, 1983

Dumpster Babies

For five years, I worked the night shift, 11:00 p.m.-7:00 a.m., once or twice a week in the infirmary at the Franciscan Missionaries of Mary. I often brought various projects from home to keep me awake when things were quiet. Opening and reading mail kept me awake and alert. One January night in 1983 I opened a letter with a picture of the inside of a big garbage Dumpster storage unit, with its huge door opened. Inside it one could see jar upon jar of baby parts from abortions.

There it was: the horror of abortion, naked and transparent for me to see. Not even a burial for these babies, human beings like you and me, just a little younger. The picture of this fact hit me between the eyes. With that picture in my memory, I could not pretend abortion was not happening on a wide scale. It became fixed in my mind's eye.

They were defenseless. These babies were totally dependent on their mothers' bodies to grow large enough to survive outside their uteruses. These babies depended on their fathers to protect their moms and themselves when they lived in their mothers' wombs.

I went to the Chapel with the Blessed Sacrament at the end of the hall and prayed for the babies, their parents, and all of us, as I listened for the sick sisters call bells to ring for my help.

In a short time...In seven short months, I learned that:

- Mother Teresa of Calcutta's faith, love and indomitable will have set an example of compassionate generosity that awakens the conscience of the world.

- We are created in an explosion of love by our loving God.
- An abortion doctor hates Christians because they know God forgives them. He believes God will never forgive him for what he does.
- My friend was offered an abortion like a cup of coffee.
- It takes courage to carry a child.
- God is a stern warrior of love.
- The gaze of Christ's love melts our hearts. His gaze of forgiveness transformed Peter's shame into the security of experiencing that he was loved unconditionally.
- Pope John Paul II, who survived an assassination attempt, forgave his assassin and called the world to pray for reconciliation.
- A garbage dumpster was full of aborted babies.

"What's next?" I wondered.

NOVENA

FEBRUARY, 1983

On the kitchen counter at the Franciscan Infirmary, someone left a novena prayer card to St. Theresa of the Child Jesus, also known as St. Theresa, The Little Flower. I prayed the following prayer for nine days, asking God to send people to take care of women and men suffering after abortion:

"My Novena Rose Prayer
O Little Theresa of the Child Jesus, please pick for me a rose from the Heavenly gardens and send it to me as a message of love.

O Little Flower of Jesus, ask God today to grant the favors I now place with confidence in your hands....

(*Mention specific requests*)
Please send people to help women and men suffering after abortion, and please help the suffering ones recover.

St. Theresa, help me to always believe as you did, in God's great love for me, so that I might imitate your 'Little Way' each day. Amen."

I had no idea that helping people recover after abortion would eventually become my job. I went about my business caring for my family, preparing for a Master's degree in nursing, praying at the retreat house, and working one night a week at the Infirmary.

CHAPTER III

TESTING THE HUNCH
1983

Once my personal journey and the hunch that many people probably are suffering after abortion blended, the hunch needed testing. Part of the testing came through my ordinary life situations and events. Part came through 1) conversations with three other couples in our parish, the friends whose party we went to while Jack and I were on retreat, 2) conversations with other friends, 3) letters from "experts" I wrote to, like Robert Coles of Harvard, asking for opinions about post abortion pain, 4) newspaper articles, 5) and a research paper on grief after abortion that I wrote for a graduate level counseling course.

Conversations with our parish friends often gravitated toward legalized abortion—what it is, and what it does to people. We were loving, truthful, and very respectful of each other and all other people whether they were involved in abortion or not. We cared as much for the abortion doctor as for ourselves. We tried to understand the whole picture.

I did not know it at the time but one of the women in our discussion group had had an abortion years earlier. Another one of us knew it and said to me carefully, "You never know who has had an abortion.

You would be surprised. There are people you know who have." I didn't ask who.

His words inspired me to be even more careful of what I said and how I said it. I could say what I needed to say as long as it was with love and great respect.

As Father John Powell, S.J. says in his book *Abortion the Silent Holocaust:* "Love is the only way to go."

"As I sift through my own priorities and values, I consider that the fundamental option of my life is that I have chosen to make love the motive of my life. I want my life and all that I do somehow to be an act of love. Of course, I am fragile and I fail, but this is my ideal, my life wager. At all the crossroads of life and in all the moments of decision, I want only to ask: What is the loving thing to do, to be, to say? So I want my pro-life stance to be an act of love. Anger, hatred and vengeance are sirens of seduction which can only mislead us.

Anger eats away at the angry; hatred destroys the hater. Vengeance is a psychological cancer. Negative motivation and emotions wear out. They end in bitterness. As a motive and emotion, love is susceptible of continual growth. It blossoms into beauty not bitterness."

In our discussion group, we each had a copy of the *Roe v. Wade* decision. We tried to study and understand it. In our meetings in each other's homes we hashed over the prob-lems and is-sues. Some topics we discussed were:

On what basis did the U.S. Supreme Court decide to rule in favor of legalized abortion?

Where does this leave the babies? Where are they now? Are they in limbo? What is limbo? What happens to their souls? What happens to their bodies? Are they buried? Bob, a member of our group, said he knew a funeral director who goes to the hospital and provides a proper burial for some babies who have no names. "It is very sad for him but it helps him find hope by doing something for them."

What about forgiveness for abortion? What's the Church's position and teaching on this? What about repentance, healing and forgiveness that is the mission of Christ? Is abortion the unforgivable sin?

What can we do to help? If people don't dare talk about having an abortion, are some suffering in silence?

Why are people doing abortions? What happens to teens and young people who think that a Supreme Court decision is a sanction, that it must be OK if it's within the law? What about our own children? How can we protect them from this?

What do people know about their bodies and reproduction? Do they know what they are doing?

And then our values and feelings came out too. "I'm scared." "Each day, with each abortion more people are touched by them. One abortion ripples through a family, a circle of friends and acquaintances. One abortion impacts a whole lot of people."

What concerned me was the actual suffering that a woman goes through after an abortion. I knew, from believing my mother's death was my fault, how it feels to be out of it because something down deep keeps gnawing at you. I also know this gnawing tiger doesn't go away until it is addressed. Stuffing things takes a lot of energy. It takes a lot of it to keep the lid on, and the lid is never secure. These emotions find other ways to come out. And I know so well how hard it is to understand all this without someone's help identifying and defining it all. Suppression is a scary thing. Once the original event that caused trauma is forgotten, it's possible to partially die inside. But the tiger inside rumbles around with energy of its own, needing attention, trying to express its need for help. The tiger is a deep wound that will not go away. Trying to help people recover from the deep wound of abortion before they forget what happened to them makes sense to me.

My course was set. I had plenty to think about as I did my household chores and took care of my family. I kept getting signals and thoughts about people to talk with, books and articles to read, and avenues to explore. In different ways I kept sensing the Lord wanted his merciful heart to be known for those suffering after abortion.

Instead of quietly being in the background of things, supporting and encouraging others to do their jobs, this calling put me in a new role, that of initiator. It was both exciting and very difficult. I learned that I could not assume that someone else would take the lead, because they were not going to. I talked it all over with Jack every step of the way, and he was very helpful. I could not have done any of this without him. But this was my idea, my hunch. If it was going to go anywhere, I had to give it birth. I had to be the one to bring it up and talk with others about it. I was in the hot seat and I had to be faithful, even when I felt crazy myself for introducing something so painful that nobody really wanted to think about it. In reality, partly what I had to bring to others was the sad news that a huge number of people are suffering right under our noses and they are in too much pain to say so. The good news I could bring was a message of hope that Our Lord wants to be at the center of helping everyone through this.

I called my friend, Steve Burke, a social worker, and a fellow parishioner who was Director of the Office of Family Life, in the Diocese of Providence. I asked if I could talk over an idea with him.

"Of course," he said. So we explored helping people who are suffering after abortion. Steve offered to help in any way he could and then said: "This is very important. Stay with it. Steady at the helm wins the race!" He said this to me many more times!

The next person I approached was a Roman Catholic priest, Father Jude McGeough. I knew the Church's mission is to bring forgiveness. Priests hear our confessions in the Sacrament of Reconciliation. I needed to question a priest about confession after abortion. Father Jude was saying Mass in our parish one Sunday, and he gave a moving homily about God's mercy. I had known Father Jude for years and knew him to be compassionate. After Mass, I approached him and asked two bold questions: "Do many women who have had abortions come to you for confession?" And, "How would you respond to a woman who came to you for confession after an abortion?" I told him: "I'm asking because I am concerned about women after abortion and what they go through and how they can find help." Father Jude's answer was compassionate and merciful. He was willing to discuss the issue with me more, so we made an appointment. After sharing my journey thus far with him, he said, "Plan a meeting with others. I'd like to travel with this concern."

Diane Manning, who was a woman highly respected by my husband, yet unknown to me, was my next sharing companion. Sister Kieran Flynn suggested I contact Diane, the mother of a large family, who was a prayerful, good, kind person and who was active in the Church and the community. She was concerned about many issues of our day.

As we got to know each other, Diane told me that many years earlier, while watching the David Suskind Show, she was baffled to hear some women speaking of "the meaningful experience of abortion." She thought "Something is very wrong here." Diane had been involved in pro-life work ever since, and she was very interested in providing healing for women who have had an abortion.

Diane and I began to meet, pray and explore what we could do to help people troubled after abortion. Then we began meeting as a group with Steve and Father Jude and eventually became the founding board of After Abortion Helpline.

ARTICLES AND STORIES

At first we concentrated on educating ourselves by reading articles and stories that came to our attention.

Diane gave me a beautiful five page article titled "Post Abortion Reconciliation and Pastoral Care," by Rev. Edward M. Bryce. The author expressed the heart of what I was after... *reconciliation*, or forgiveness for abortion and care for those suffering after abortion. At the end of the article there were program resources and names of people we could contact for help and advice. I wrote these people and waited for their answers.

I was hungry for information and Jack kept finding articles in various papers and bringing them home for me to study.

One article was in the *Wall Street Journal,* in the summer of 1983. The title read: "Japanese Ceremonies Show Previous Doubts Over Use Of Abortion. Rituals Atone For Guilt but Mixed Feelings Lead to Public Debate." The article went on to say: "Many Japanese women who have had abortions say they feel guilty and ashamed; some who have had them earlier report reoccurring bad dreams." The article went on to say that a Buddhist Monk explained that their feelings are prompted more by an emotional response than religious or philosophical beliefs. He also said many would go to a Buddhist Temple out of town to erect statues in atonement for their aborted babies.

This article confirmed for me the reality of suffering after abortion. It strengthened my hunch that women do suffer after abortion. It may seem odd that I needed confirmation of this suffering since it probably is obvious to people who are suffering after abortion. But having not had an abortion myself, I needed to back up my very strong common sense hunch with facts.

As the picture of post abortion pain became clearer, I envisioned a huge problem of public health proportions. I had to paddle through a great sea of silence. I felt like a salmon swimming up the river rapids to spawn and die but I wasn't planning to die. I had to keep going to discover a way to help people suffering after abortion even if people didn't believe me or didn't want to or couldn't grasp the reality of post-abortion pain. I knew, I just knew. I even went to a day-long conference at Brown University on Depression in Women, to see if abortion would be mentioned as a cause of depression. It was not mentioned.

Several levels of purpose were operating in me as I pursued healing and forgiveness for abortion. One was the loss of my mother and my own post traumatic grief and guilt. Another was my spiritual quest of forgiveness and healing after abortion. And professionally, my nursing formation made me feel responsible. I had been a public health nurse, visiting families in poor neighborhoods in New Haven, Connecticut, teaching them newborn care, among other things.

As I followed leads in this uncharted area of helping, my educational training demanded I be clear, valid and impeccable in my sources of information. I had to prove my point so I would be credible to others in this very sensitive area. I over-prepared myself and those in our helping group. We had to prove worthy and credible to have the right to help others.

On June 4, 1983, Jack noticed a little piece in the *Providence Journal* describing a program called "Support After Abortion," in Youngstown, Ohio. As I read it, I felt just great learning that someone out there was working on this. I wrote for information.

In July, 1983, one night at work at the Franciscan Missionaries of Mary Infirmary, I found an article titled "Forgiveness For Abortion" by Sister Mary Ann Walsh in *Catholic Digest* magazine. It had tons of information such as: "millions of women suffer from guilt over abortions. Their guilt increases with age (and is heightened). It comes with subsequent pregnancies and on the anniversary of the abortion itself." It went on to discuss how and why the Church needs to be forgiveness for abortion. Sister Mary Ann was saying what I was thinking... the Church does need to be known as forgiving for abortion.

I thought that the Church offers forgiveness for abortion, but wondered how can we announce this so people who have separated themselves from the Church will know it? Where do we begin? I realized there is much more to think about and pray about now.

Some of my relatives have given me great examples of service. A distant cousin unknowingly inspired me. She was a medical doctor who pioneered services for abused children in New Hampshire. I thought *if she can do that, I can do this.*

I also knew something about my family history from the stories Dad loved to tell us. My great-great Grandmother wanted to be a nurse during the Civil War so she could take care of the soldiers but she was not allowed to because she was too young. Instead she taught the kitchen help to read so they could properly set up food trays. My great Uncle John Rockwell, M.D. lost two fingers from radiation burns as he pioneered developing the X-Ray machine. My mom was known for helping friends and relatives. She left college to take care of her mother who had TB. Mom graduated later from Smith College.

My paternal Grandmother, Grandmary, was one of the first woman professors at the University of Rhode Island, then called Rhode Island College. Her family homestead was part of the Underground Railroad, a home that hid and helped free slaves.

Also the principal of my girls' high school regularly told us we must always help others, that we had to be leaders in society as we had received so much ourselves, and been so privileged.

Another bunch of articles and stories came my way, more Markings of Mercy.

A few significant stories and subjects appeared in *Catholic Twin Circle*, on August14, 1983, under the heading*"BABY BLUES , The Psychological Effects of Abortion,"* by Mary Meehan. The article begins with:

Return to Sender
"The night I got back from Planned Parenthood, I called my best friend and was crying. I told her that I wanted my baby back. I . . . saw the doctor throw my baby in a trash can. And that tore me up. Now I think that my baby is piled under all kinds of trash. I wish now that I never had my abortion.

My family and friends tell me to put the past behind me--forget about it. But I can't. There is always that scar in my heart, that my baby is dead."

So said a 15-year-old, writing to a counselor at a pregnancy aid center. She added, "I wish that I would have found out about your center. I could have come in and talked to somebody."

Mary Meehan goes on to write:
Other girls and women are disturbed by their abortion experience, but want to put it behind them quickly and not think or talk about it, according to Linda Bird Franke who interviewed hundreds of women for her book, *The Ambivalence of Abortion.* One young woman told Franke: 'It's much easier not to think about the fetus. After all, the world would be a lot better place if there were fewer babies in it. That's the important thing.' The same woman, describing her second abortion, said that 'I didn't think of it as killing a baby but like an operation on my arm or something.' Franke writes, 'The experience of counselors and psychiatrists suggests that women who try to repress their abortion experience may be setting themselves up for long-term psychological problems.'

Denyse Handler, a Canadian pro-life activist, recently noted that 'the primary psychological reactions to an abortion are grief and guilt. These should not be considered in themselves unhealthy; they are quite natural.' But, said Handler, such feelings 'are prevented in cases where it is socially unacceptable to mourn the aborted child, to talk about the child or express regret.' She said that telling a woman who has had an abortion not to think about it, or that she could not have coped with a baby, tends 'to censor rather than air the feelings of the grieving woman. Thus she may become stuck at the level of grief or guilt and fail to work through it to a resolution.'

Regarding men and abortion, Mary Meehan goes on to say:
Elise Rose, a pro-life feminist from Kansas, speaks of men as 'having abortions.' By this she suggests that a man whose unborn child is aborted shares in the responsibility for abortion and may suffer anxiety, guilt and grief as a result.

Jack came home from work, on August 18, 1983, and told me he heard a man named Russell tell this heart-wrenching story on the car radio. I asked Jack to write it up for me, it was such an amazing story.

RUSSELL

The following story was broadcast over Station WEAN in Providence on August 18, 1983. Russell called in to a morning talk show concerning men's feelings about abortion.

Russell is over 70 years old. In 1942 he had an affair with an unmarried Norwegian girl which resulted in the girl becoming pregnant. Russell was married. The girl came from a very straight laced family. Both Russell and his friend decided that the only solution was an abortion.

Russell made arrangements with a doctor in California. When they arrived, the doctor explained that his nurse was not working that day and asked if Russell would assist him. Russell agreed and witnessed the birth of a beautiful, six months old, blond baby boy. When the baby was born, the doctor asked Russell to turn his back and then proceeded to kill the child.

Both Russell and the girl were totally devastated by the experience. They agreed never to see each other again.

Overcome with guilt Russell decided to tell his wife. She reacted with love and sympathy. She told her husband that if she had known about it, she would gladly have agreed to raise the child as her own.

Subsequently, Russell and his wife adopted four children.

Russell told the talk show host that even after forty years he still feels a great burden of guilt. He was sobbing and overcome by emotion before he finished telling the story - which he had never told anyone, except his wife."

On September 26, 1983 Jack brought home the following article from *Time Magazine*, by John Leo, p. 78, entitled *"SHARING THE PAIN OF ABORTION - Men feel isolated, angry at themselves and their partners."* It was a book review of *Men and Abortion; Lessons, Losses and Love,* by Arthur Shostak, Gary McLouth and Lynn Seng, to be published in 1984 by Praeger. The highlights were:

"A few weeks after the end of the affair, sociologist, Arthur Shostak, boarded a train in Philadelphia with his former lover and accompanied her to an abortion clinic in the suburbs. Both were in favor of the operation, but Shostak was totally unprepared for the experience. He was still enraged over an earlier comment by a clinic staffer referring to the abortion as 'the disposal of a clump of tissue.' There was no counseling or literature for males, and the clinic barred him from the operating and recovery rooms. 'I was in shock,' he recalls. 'Abortion is a man's issue too, and there is almost no one to help the million men who go through it every year.'

Since then, Shostak has spent almost ten years studying the impact of abortion on men. His conclusion: abortion is a great, unrecognized trauma for males, perhaps the only major one that most men go through without help. Shostak, a professor at Philadelphia's Drexel University, surveyed a thousand male "abortion veterans" in eighteen states who had accompanied their wives or girlfriends to abortion clinics. The survey, which will be the basis of a book, showed that most of the men felt isolated, angry at themselves and their partners, and fearful of physical and emotional damage to the women. Three quarters of the men had discussed the abortion only with the woman involved, partly out of a desire to protect her privacy, partly because they were not accustomed to expressing strong emotions.

In most cases, the pregnancy should not have come as a surprise: almost 60% of the men said they and their partners had not used contraceptives or had relied on such relatively ineffective methods as withdrawal or rhythm. Although 93% of the men said they would do all they could to avoid future abortions, 30% were repeaters who had been there before."

These are a few of the stories and articles about post-abortion suffering that give a good picture of its reality. I consider them all a gift. They gave us enough information to go forward and plan a helping service.

CHAPTER IV

THE DEVELOPMENT AND BIRTH OF AFTER ABORTION HELPLINE, INC. 1983-1985

PREGNANCY AFTERMATH HELPLINE

After studying the materials we had accumulated, Steve, Father Jude, Diane and I began to plan our service. Pregnancy Aftermath Helpline, Inc. seemed like a reasonable model for us. Pregnancy Aftermath Helpline is a free, 24-hour telephone helpline based in Milwaukee, Wisconsin, for people who are having problems or questions following a pregnancy which ends in abortion, miscarriage, or adoption placement. Its operations began November 1, 1976. Volunteer counselors answer open-ended calls from persons contacting the Helpline. A summary data sheet was kept on every call.

"Sharon," a member of our group who had an abortion, and understood the need to have someone willing to listen to the pain of those who have experienced abortion, suggested we provide a service just for post-abortion people, instead of all pregnancy losses, as Pregnancy Aftermath Helpline did. "There is no service for us here," Sharon said. We agreed with her and focused the service we were creating on post-abortion helping.

Marbeth Foley from Pregnancy Aftermath Helpline help
a lot. She shared training literature with us, including a book ﹍ur
therapist advisor, Monte Liebman, M.D., wrote on helping people. I
remember a thrilling phone call with Marbeth on July 3, 1984, when
she explained how their group was able to help their callers. In fact, I
was in heaven talking with this kind, good person who was actually
doing what we wanted to do and had vast experience and knowledge.
Marbeth shared important helping steps which we incorporated into
our training program.

We named our service After Abortion Helpline. We began all meetings with the following universal Prayer of St. Francis of Assisi:

PRAYER FOR PEACE
Lord, make me an instrument of your peace.
Where there is hatred,
let me sow love;
Where there is injury, pardon;
Where there is doubt, faith;
Where there is despair, hope;
Where there is darkness, light;
Where there is sadness, joy.

O Divine master, grant that I
may seek not so much to be consoled
as to console; to be understood as to
understand; to be loved as to love;
for it is in giving that we receive;
it is in pardoning that we are
pardoned, and it is in dying that
we are born to Eternal Life.

Amen

"Philosophy and Purpose," "We Believes,""Services We Provide." Steve Burke led us through the basic steps of developing our non-profit social service agency. Steve's social work background, counseling experience, and years of telephone helping experience on the Birthright phone line, gave him the tools to lead us. He helped us create our "Philosophy and Purpose," our "We Believes…," and the "Services We Provide." They are as follows:

STATEMENT OF PHILOSOPHY AND PURPOSE

Many women who have had abortions regret that decision either immediately or later. We hope to provide some help for these women, and for any other people who have been affected by the decision.

We Believe That:

A relationship begins to develop between parent and child in the womb.

Severing this relationship through abortion at any stage of pregnancy can carry pain that is often ignored or denied.

Recovery from this pain requires facing grief and other emotions, and dealing with them.

Any person can come to freedom, wholeness and reconciliation with God, self, the child, and others.

SERVICES WE PROVIDE

After Abortion Helpline, Inc. is a free, confidential, non-sectarian telephone service, using trained lay volunteers, who assist women and men in dealing with the after effects of abortion. Our purpose is to encourage women and men to mobilize their inner strengths, resolve their conflicts, and restore their lives. We also offer referral services for medical, spiritual and counseling help when needed.

Once we got this done, the legal tasks could proceed. Jack, my husband, with his knowledge of the law, wrote our incorporation papers, our application for 501(c)(3) IRS non-profit status, and our constitution and by-laws. We also obtained an IRS taxpayer ID number.

Our working group became a formal board of directors, which grew as time went on to include a mix of Christian people from several different churches, men and women, and one Jewish psychiatrist. Some were party to an abortion and some were not. We were housewives, professional counselors, nurses, social workers, a priest, a psychiatrist and a lawyer.

When our 501(c)(3) probationary acceptance letter came, we were free to begin raising tax deductible start-up funds and apply for a start-up grant.

TRAINING PROGRAM - RECRUITING VOLUNTEERS

At the same time we developed a training program and, with that in place, we recruited volunteers. I prayed a lot for this. Who could we find who cared enough about people suffering after abortion to train, commit to the Helpline, then take a weekly three-hour telephone shift helping people troubled after abortion? As I prayed, people would come to mind who might make good volunteers. In an in-depth interview, I talked with each one about our Helpline and asked them to consider training and becoming a Helpline volunteer. Everyone had to accept our "Philosophy and Purpose," "We Believes," and "Services We Provide," and be willing to complete the training program. It was understood that our own families' needs came first, if we had to miss a meeting or get a substitute for our phone shift.

Our little group expanded as we called on the expertise of many people. Marion Walters, who was in charge of Rhode Island volunteer training at Samaritans, the international suicide hotline, was incredibly helpful in training us. I came across an inspiring story in our newspaper about The Samaritans, so I called them and spoke with Marion. Samaritan volunteers "befriend" their callers. Marion adapted some of their methods to our telephone service, and helped us see how to get to the nitty-gritty bottom line of helping a person in crisis on the phone, caring for the caller, and being their friend on the phone for as long as they needed us. Marion was a beautiful person and she inspired us all.

Many other professionals also helped us design and give the training, and we gathered a great deal more post-abortion literature to draw upon.

SYNOPSIS OF TRAINING PROGRAM

Our twenty plus hour training program was designed to:

Sharpen volunteers' non-judgmental listening skills.
Inform volunteers of the common reactions after abortion.
Prepare volunteers to be trained helpers, not counselors, who will not give advice.
Prepare volunteers to refer callers to the ministers, rabbis, priests, doctors, counselors, or social service agencies on the referral list.

We used a text, *Giving and Taking Help*, by Alan Keith Lucas, and other educational materials, and we spent time beyond the twenty hours doing supervised practicum work.

The topics we covered were:

Telephone helping: what can I expect?
Listening - Samaritan "Befriending."
Common reactions after abortion: psychological, spiritual, and medical, including conception, pregnancy, delivery, and abortion procedures.
Grief work after abortion.
Basic issues in telephone helping.
Volunteer supervision and the ongoing support system.
Internal operations, policies, etc.

Our instructors, a medical doctor, three therapists, and some clergy, were experienced, competent professionals.

SOME MAIN TRAINING POINTS

We did **self-work**, which means looking at and acknowledging our own issues so we could be fully present to a caller. We learned to separate our own issues from theirs so we could stay with them on the phone for their sakes and not fall apart ourselves because of something the caller said that triggered something in us, such as our own abortion, our own encounter with the death of a child, or of a parent (as in my case). Understanding that we were all vulnerable and that we had our own painful memories was important. It was very helpful to be able to know when something triggered such a memory in us, that it was not a pain the other person had, but our own. We could listen more clearly to the other person and tell ourselves we'd take care of ourselves later in regard to this. Our purpose in doing this self work was to prepare well to receive each caller and to be helpful.

Listening well is so important. Persons in distress need to hear themselves say out loud what is inside them. As a person hears himself/herself say things that surface about the abortion to someone who truly listens, connections are made inside the person...private, sacred connections that begin the healing process. It is essential to have someone who will listen well, allow long silences for making these connections, and to allow long, loud sobs, or, just plain crying.

The well of pain is very deep and the first connection with that pain can be earth-shattering. The person carrying that pain deserves a compassionate, honest listener to validate the pain and to validate the reality of the abortion, the trauma that caused the pain. Then healing can begin. Most callers are women and the willingness to listen creates a bond.

Our caller may feel she will cry forever, that if she starts she won't be able to stop. We can tell her she is not alone, that many callers say the same thing. We can assure her she is not the only one experiencing this turmoil, and that what she is experiencing is normal for someone who has had an abortion. We can tell her she is not crazy, as she believes she is, but that her reaction is healthy, for she has been holding in a grief too horrible to bear, and yet she has had to, because it's a forbidden grief few want to talk about or honestly admit exists.

Knowing she is not alone is a great relief to our caller. A tiny glimmer of hope begins to dawn at that point. She can go on to give details, to identify what happened if she chooses, or to say whatever she needs to say about it all.

We give the caller as much **time** as needed. Often an hour is enough, but many times a caller can only handle a few minutes. The time is controlled by the caller who is free to hang up at any time. We assure the caller that's fine, knowing she needs space to deal with all that is shifting inside her heart, mind and soul. And, we trust that process. We know this was her time to begin healing and we sense the conversation is most sacred.

During the years the Helpline was in operation, we spoke anonymously to hundreds of women and men on the phone and their relief was palpable. Their problems were not immediately over but at least they experienced a new beginning. Their relief was often expressed in a gently, whispered "thank you." Most of the time we did not know how they were doing unless they called back, but we did know they were on their way. They knew that they were free to call us back if they needed to, or to carry on with the referrals we had given them.

My friends on the Helpline and I prayed for our callers, entrusting them to God. We carried them in our hearts and prayers for a long time. We prayed during our telephone shift that we could be our very best for them. We discovered that our prayer fine tuned our gifts and love for each and every caller.

Our brochure read:

"TROUBLED
AFTER
ABORTION?
WANT TO TALK
WITH SOMEONE?

You or your friend are not alone if you feel troubled after abortion. The abortion may have happened recently or years ago.

You may feel **confused** and **isolated** by unexpected feelings which can be difficult to sort out. It's important to remember that feelings are neither right nor wrong, but can be powerful and even overwhelming.

You may have no one to talk with about your experience. Talking with someone might help you feel less troubled.
WHY STAY BURDENED?

Some common reactions after abortion are:
- Bleeding
- Sense of loss
- Guilt
- Anger
- Anxiety
- Depression
- Poor Self Image
- Isolation
- Remorse
- Fear
- Shame

Calling the Helpline may be the first step towards recovery if you are hurting. After Abortion Helpline is staffed by trained volunteers who are willing to listen.
CALL 0000000000
© by After Abortion Helpline, Inc. 1986"

I cannot give the number out because our service has retired. There are many excellent services available now. Rachel's Vineyard Hotline number is 877-HOPE-4-Me and email is rachelsvineyard.org. Project Rachel numbers can be found at most Roman Catholic Dioceses. The number for the National Office Of Post-Abortion Reconciliation And Healing, (NOPARH) is: 1-800-5-WE-CARE and email is wwwnoparh.

org/women.html. You can call Lumina, Hope and Healing after Abortion, a ray of light in abortion's darkness at 1-877-586-4621, or email @ wwwpostabortionhelp.org. And, for information or to register for Days of Prayer and Healing, call the Sisters of Life at: (toll free) 866.575.0075 or email@ sistersoflife.org.

OUR SERVICE

Our service was anonymous because most post-abortion people do not want anyone to know who they are. We respected that. We could never trace a call. This was before "caller ID." The number people called went to our Helpline phone, which was located at a telephone answering service, only for the purpose of having someone put "call forwarding" on and off the phone, to and from our homes, where we took the calls.

We took calls in our homes for three hours at a time, 11:00 a.m. to 2:00 p.m., or 7:00 p.m. to 10:00 p.m. Our families understood that during our shift they were to stay off the phone. If other people called our home, we would ask if we could call them back. Our families helped us have a dedicated line for three hours once a week. They were a vital part of the helping.

We began taking calls on November 21, 1985, the week before Thanksgiving, knowing that holidays can be difficult for people who are suffering. Callers knew about us from a little ad in the classified section of our daily paper. It said:

After Abortion Helpline, Inc
Troubled after abortion? Need to talk? May we help?
Compassionate, confidential
Call 000-0000 11:00 a.m. - 2 p.m. 7-10 p.m.

Our fourteen, plus or minus, volunteers were from all walks of life. We were women, men, young, and elderly, from different religious affiliations. Some had experienced an abortion, some had not. Our Board of Directors was a working board so most of us took a telephone shift once a week.

Dr. Irving Rosen, Associate Medical Director of Butler Hospital, Chief of the Religion and Psychiatry Program that he developed, joined our board. Jack saw the announcement of this new service in the newspaper and said I might want to call Dr. Rosen. I phoned Dr. Rosen and we made a lunch date. In the cafeteria of Butler Hospital I explained After Abortion Helpline and asked if he could help us. He said yes and invited us to hold our board meetings at the hospital. For a long time after that day Dr. Rosen conducted a post-abortion support group on Friday afternoons in the hospital.

At times when we became discouraged because we desired more people would call the Helpline, Dr. Rosen would say to us: "If you don't provide this service, who will? Nobody else is doing it now. You have to keep going."

Chapter V

CALLERS

SYNOPSIS OF CALLS

It may help to know a summary of what callers were saying during the first fourteen months of our After Abortion Helpline service. Callers were anonymous. They could make up a name for themselves or use just a first name or no name. Anonymity was crucial.

The following is a synopsis of these calls. I presented them at a paper session at the June, 1987 meeting in New Orleans of the Association of Interdisciplinary Research in Values and Social Change. That winter I had seen a "Call For Papers" from this organization in a newspaper. I gulped and said to myself, *I could do that. I could deliver a paper on what our callers were saying the first fourteen months of our service. We need to share this with others.*

I wrote the paper based on our call sheets and sent in the application. When I was accepted I was thrilled and a little scared. I had never done such a thing before. The following call reports are what I presented. The types of telephone calls we received over sixteen months, from November 21, 1985 through March 13, 1987. Of 164 calls received, 103 were from women after abortion; 16 were from men both before and after abortion; and 45 were from others.

- Most callers are Roman Catholic, in a state that is 65% Roman Catholic.
- Many callers have not been able to talk at length about bottled up feelings and reactions. They often begin timidly and progress into a more confident sharing of feelings and suffering
- Most women expressed guilt, depression, loss, confusion, regret, sorrow, change in the relationship with the man, anxiety, isolation, and loneliness.
- 32% of women called within three months after their abortion.
- 67% of women called within one year.
- 33% of women called after one year.
- Most callers expressed relief and appreciation to volunteers for listening to them. Many are relieved to know they are not the only one suffering after abortion.
- Sixteen calls were from men directly affected by abortion. Of these, ten men called after abortion. "Our relationship is going down the tubes." "We fight a lot. Is this what happens after?" "She refuses to even talk to me." "I'm no longer interested in her sexually." Two men called before abortion, concerned for their girlfriends who were contemplating abortion. "She is real nervous, crying a lot." "I'll support her either way, but the decision should be hers."
- Forty-five other calls included eight from family members concerned for a female relative after abortion. "My mother wants to talk with someone about her abortion forty years ago." One woman who encouraged her teenage daughter to abort her second pregnancy called two weeks later, (afterward) feeling victimized, angry and guilty. "I quit my job to stay home to care for her first child so she could go back to school."
- Three calls were seeking help for a friend. One caller was concerned for her son's former girlfriend who called their home repeatedly, claiming she had three abortions and was now suicidal: "She doesn't go to school--she just lies around the house all day." A father worried about his teenage daughter who was

to accompany a friend to an abortion clinic.

- Eight callers were seeking or contemplating abortion. One woman had lost a child to cystic fibrosis and was now pregnant again. Her husband and their doctors were adamant about no more children, but she did not wish to abort. Her husband was threatening to leave her.

Various impressions received from callers were:

- Callers often keep the Helpline number for a while before calling.
- Freedom to call depends on the caller's privacy or ability to talk. Often callers hang up in the middle of a conversation saying, "Someone is coming" or "I can't talk anymore." Some abruptly hang up.
- People feeling numbness are not calling.
- Those who call are trying to recover.
- Though many referrals are given, it is not known how many are acted upon.
- Many callers don't want to go back to the abortion clinic for help, saying, "I don't want to go near that place."
- Callers are secretive, depressed, shut down, isolated, and lonely. Few have someone who can listen to them, want to, or know how to. Many don't trust anyone with their double-scandal, i.e., getting pregnant, then having an abortion.
- Callers may struggle for a long time to resolve their abortion experience.

WHAT CALLERS ARE SAYING:
VOLUNTEER NARRATIVES FROM CALL SHEETS

The following narratives tell our story best. They are narratives from the call sheets we'd write up after someone called the After Abortion Helpline. We took notes during the call and we wrote them to review the call for ourselves, to help us unwind and summarize what the caller said and what we said. We also used the narratives to help each other in-service and critique how we did. During our "in-service" training meetings our group of volunteers would go over the call sheets, and Betty Jane, who was a trained counselor, would supervise us. We learned a lot from each other. And we had each other's support.

Volunteers were required to call me within 24 hours to report on a call. We wanted to be on top of each call and to be able to pass on to the next volunteer word of someone in severe distress who might call again soon.

I might mention that we also agreed to be available to each other after a shift, meaning we could call another volunteer and talk through what happened in a call and get insight, critique and support. We tried to remind each other of aspects of our training that applied to our call. Often we felt we had failed, only to be reminded of a positive by a fellow volunteer.

The reports of the calls we received tell the story best about what our loving merciful God was doing among us, how much love flowed through these dedicated volunteers, and how beautiful each caller is in her or his struggle for truth and healing in her or his life.

I have changed the names in these call sheets to fictitious names, and omitted some possibly identifying information. The following stories are taken from notes from volunteers' call sheets. They were not meant to be written up in complete sentences.

A WOMAN IN HER TWENTIES

A difficult complex situation, loss of babies (her words), loss of lover, loss of friends, betrayal of friends, betrayal of self. - deeply grieving- -not interested in a clergy referral - interfering with work, very lonely, very isolated- -caller very articulate about feelings, but did not realize she was grieving human losses-'It has been a month since my boyfriend took off with my close girlfriend and I am ready to start feeling better now.'

- mourning interfering with work - everyone presuming she's

upset just at boyfriend-extremely hurt and betrayed by boyfriend-felt she had both abortions to please him, to keep him. She did not want either.

- Could not recall many details of second abortion & this upset her. 'It feels like a black hole' especially since she had decided to have the second abortion by herself. Lover gave no support with either pregnancy.

- Said she felt she could forgive herself for the first abortion but not the second. Felt she had to 'Make it up to the babies'; had 'weird' feelings about needing to have a baby by the lover in order to accomplish this, but on the other hand wanted no more to do with him.

- However still seeing the 'lover' on occasion, felt she was still in love with him-love/hate feelings. Caller seemed to have a lot of suppressed anger toward him.

- extremely lonely- lost all her friends when she broke up with lover. Very significant to her, not close to family either. I encouraged her to seek out at least a couple of friends -v. afraid of rejection.

- She asked about counseling, had little $ for counseling, took a phone # but said she would probably work it out herself.

- Wished someone had talked her out of having the second abortion. "I hardened my heart. I shut down my feelings." -Wanted to see the 'jar' after her second abortion but was not allowed. -I encouraged her to see a Doctor about a gyn problem, did not want to go back to - - Assoc. And she did not want to tell anyone about the 2 abortions.

TEENAGE FEMALE
THANKSGIVING DAY

Caller asked for a place to get counseling. Her mother went with her when she had abortion. She is living at home, going to school. She said very little, I had to keep asking questions to prod her on.

She saw movie on television about abortion and it has bothered her since then. She has not discussed this with anyone. She is having fetal pain concern. Boy knew about it - they broke up because he was a "jerk."

Self Evaluation: had to "drag out" information as to why she called- she is troubled now as a result of seeing the movie on abortion-at the time she wanted to do it and her mother agreed with her. She was two months pregnant.

I told her she was wise to want help and she should be free of this guilt feeling. She didn't respond much - just saying she wished she hadn't done it.

Referral or expected outcome: Don't know if she will follow up on counseling. I told her to call again if she wasn't finding the right spot for her.

A FEMALE IN EARLY THIRTIES WHO HAD AN ABORTION SIX YEARS AGO

A woman called complaining of depression. She had a hysterectomy. She did not admit to any religious affiliation.

I had a hang up and an hour later this call came. She talked quite a long time and said that around the holidays was the hardest time. She needed to talk to someone.

MOTHER OF DAUGHTER WHO HAD AN ABORTION

Mother of woman in late thirties called to try and find help for her daughter. Mother reports her daughter had abortion twelve years ago but seems to be suffering effects in worsening degree with each succeeding pregnancy. The daughter has three young children.

Daughter has never discussed the abortion with anyone in the family except for a vague, passing remark to a brother. Parents want to bring up abortion issue but are afraid it will cause her to have a nervous breakdown. Mother reports the daughter has been in Butler Hospital (a local psychiatric hospital) and has had various bouts with mental illness since the abortion.

Mother was very unsure of what direction to take. I asked her what was the worst possible thing that could happen if she brought up abortion. We talked through this, and concluded that she would try to reach daughter's therapist and discuss her own observations about daughter's abortion. Also gave a priest's number and encouraged her to call us back for more help.

WOMAN, AGE 18-24, ABORTION THREE MONTHS AGO AT NINE WEEKS GESTATION

Calling because of suicidal thoughts, medical problems, relationship disruption Sense that client is unable at this time to deal with the experience beyond a very primitive, basic level. Realize this is causing major life disruption, asks about fetal pain, etc, but unable to describe experience except in bits and pieces, halted when asked about doctor, abortion itself. She is in denial. She ended the call at this point. She asked about more peripheral issues earlier.

She expresses guilt. Is angry at mother and boyfriend, Church, close to Christmas. She called clinic about pain. Is seeing pieces- visions, images of dead baby. Awful, had felt "I would die immediately after abortion and ever since. Medical- bleeding- Tylenol and antibiotics given by clinic. She did not return to clinic third time for follow-up- still bleeding occasionally. Suicidal -has Valium pills. She had thoughts of suicide Friday night. Caller is afraid of her own pain.

Felt she couldn't admit to mother she'd aborted. Felt could not talk with priest. I talked about healing with time, possibility of healing in future and about other women who have been healed, etc. She did not respond to this. I gave many medical and spiritual suggestions for action – she could not even say the word (abortion). "I should have known better," she said.

TWO CALLS AND A VISIT

Virginia's daughter called in February, 1986. Virginia had an abortion forty years ago in another country. Virginia's dog died recently and that triggered her memories of the abortion. Virginia spoke to me briefly but wanted her daughter to speak for her.

Her daughter called the Helpline because Virginia saw an article about After Abortion Helpline, with a picture of three of us, in the *Providence Journal*, on January 18, 1986, and our telephone number. Her mother wanted to speak to me in person as I looked like the oldest in the group. She did not want anyone to know about the abortion. Another volunteer told her when I would be on duty so she could speak to me.

I saw Virginia at my house as a friend who wanted to talk about something. In my home she told me her story and she talked at length about how tormented she is regarding the abortion. We related on a spiritual level as Virginia expressed her need as spiritual. "Show me how to get out of this torment," she had said. "Show me how to do it. My conscience condemns me." A friend had given her a tape on forgiving self. I sent her home with a Lynn Brothers tape and companion book. Both were called *Praying With Another For Healing*. One chapter in the book and part of the tape was about "Diane" and her healing after abortion.

A few weeks later, Virginia called the Helpline. I was on duty. Her presenting problem this day was this: she stated she was tormented, woke up trembling, unable to concentrate, needed to talk. We talked for an hour. Her story again was one of self-torment. She knows God forgives her but she can't forgive herself. Believes this state she's in is destroying her – She thinks she is destroying herself.

Also Virginia has medical problems.

I told Virginia she had been a gift for me because she had shared her pain with me. I had been going through some of my own pain and her pain had helped me some weeks after our visit. The fact that she had been a help gave her hope. "That's what we need, to love each other and help each other," she said.

Virginia agreed to put away the harsh judgmental Old Testament quotes that kept tormenting her mind. "Satan really throws them at me. I know that from listening to an evangelist on TV who helps me understand this," she said.

I read part of Psalm 139 to Virginia:

"Truly you have formed my inmost being;
you knit me in my mother's womb.
I give you thanks that I am fearfully, wonderfully made;
wonderful are your works." V. 13,14

"How weighty are your designs, O God;
how vast the sum of them!
Were I to recount, they would outnumber the sands;
did I reach the end of them, I should still
be with you." V. 16, 17

RSV translation

I suggested that Virginia ask God for the grace to experience His love for her and to pray this Psalm, or any part of it. At this, Virginia seemed a little more mobilized.

RACHEL

A thirty-year-old, married, Jewish woman named Rachel, called on a Tuesday afternoon, at 1:00, in March, 1987. She had an abortion the previous October and wanted a referral for abortion counseling. The United Way referred her to us.

Rachel requested an "abortion counselor" who had experience of abortion. Said she was in therapy and therapist felt ill-equipped to handle this issue. The therapist suggested she find someone else to help her. She had called a series of people, Jewish Community Services, Rape Crisis Center (pregnancy was *not* a result of rape) and finally United Way, who gave her our name. Said her therapist suggested she would need 3-6 sessions to deal with abortion issue.

Told her I didn't know of a particular therapist who "specialized" in post-abortion counseling or support groups other than WEBA (Women Exploited By Abortion). Told Rachel I would have S. From WEBA call her (Rachel gave me her name and telephone number.)

Felt she was angrier at boyfriend for bailing out than she was upset about the abortion. She talked a lot about him. However, she did say she was concerned that this may have been her only chance to have a baby and now she has ruined it. She has not had a period since abortion (Oct. '86) but is seeing a gynecologist.

Called S. with info. S. will suggest a specific counselor to her.

Feelings and reactions expressed by this caller were: need to talk, guilt, anger, sense of loss, change in relationship with the man, confusion.

JILL (FIRST OF TWO CALLS)

In February of 1986, a twenty-plus-year-old Roman Catholic woman called to talk about how sad she felt after her abortion three months ago. "I feel so sad. I feel I will never be happy again," Jill said.

She was very hesitant at first. Spoke with a definite accent (I later learned she is from another country, and was married in Rhode Island.) She feels very alone here. Husband insisted on abortion - said he "never wanted kids." When Jill married, she thought he just didn't want children right away. Since abortion, has turned against husband and left him two weeks ago and moved to an apartment. She does not drive. I determined where she lives. Feels totally alienated from God and the church. Knows she could never go to a priest "back home" because they are so severe. I spoke to her about God's mercy. She said she felt "terrible" about what she had done and couldn't understand why her husband couldn't share her feelings. The only person she is close to in R.I. is her husband's cousin who helped her move, but doesn't know about the abortion. The only other person who knows about the abortion is a sister back home whom she called. She wants very much to return to her family, but feels she will never be able to go back since the abortion. Her sister agrees that she should not return home.

Jill asked a lot of questions. "Will I ever forget?" "Do other women go through this etc?" She didn't seem anxious to speak with other women who have had abortions, however. She came to R.I. to attend a local college, where she is presently a part-time student. But she "can't go back to school. I can't face anybody."

Before I realized where she lived and her transportation difficulties,

I had suggested she call Fr. F., who speaks her language and also would be helpful to counsel her on her marriage problems. She had said she feels much more comfortable speaking in her language.

After realizing where she lived I suggested she walk to a nearby church and talk with a certain priest there. She seemed agreeable to following both suggestions. Jill was a lovely person - very sweet and sensitive. I promised to pray for her and told her she could call the Helpline again any time, but that I would be "on" again on Fridays from 11-2.

Jill had to go to the hospital for repairs after complications (bleeding) developed after the abortion at an abortion clinic. Physically she's alright now.

Feelings and reactions expressed by the caller were: "Need to talk, guilt, depression, sense of loss, sorrow/grief, change in relationship w/ man, regret, loss of self-esteem, betrayal, family problems, marital problems.

JILL (SECOND OF TWO CALLS)

On May 23, 1986, three months after Jill's last call, Jill called to tell me she was returning home to her country. She had attempted to reconcile with her husband and was pregnant again. Would never have another abortion and hasn't told her husband about the pregnancy because she is afraid he would insist on another abortion. Said she had been very unhappy in R.I. but was very grateful for After Abortion Helpline and couldn't leave without calling to say goodbye to me.

Jill has never spoken with a priest. She tried on several occasions to reach Fr. J. I suggested again she try Fr. F. She has tremendous guilt that God will punish her for her abortion by having something go wrong with the baby she was carrying. I tried to reassure her that this was unlikely - and that worrying would be no good for either her or the child.

I really pray she can speak to a priest before she leaves. She is terrified of the priests in her village at home.

Lovely person - continue to pray for her.

BOYFRIEND

On December 16, 1985 a twenty-plus-year -"Boyfriend" called at 9:00 p.m. concerned about his girlfriend. He was raised Catholic, she was raised Methodist.

The girlfriend broke up with him. He's worried about her and was missing her. She's feeling a lot of anger toward him and a lot of denial over the abortion. He's wondering how he can help her. She sounds very isolated, not telling anyone, not wanting to discuss it. She left him after attending a baby shower for a friend which was around the time when her baby would have been born. He did not want the abortion but left the decision up to her and said he will support her in any decision. Even though they had been living together and talking marriage <u>he</u> did not want to marry and have the baby together - excuses; still in school, couldn't support a family etc. He did seem very caring about her and lonely without her. She is now refusing to see him, became very angry towards him on the phone after he had written to her about the abortion.

Caller did not seem to relate to the abortion in a personal way, as far as this being his child too. He said he went with her when she had it. Mostly he was concerned about her. The caller began to drink heavily when she left and hospitalized himself because of it. I assured him, his girlfriend's behavior was normal as this is a very difficult time.

Feelings and reactions expressed by caller are: anxiety, depression, sense of loss, isolation and loneliness.

Chapter VI

CONFERENCES: A TURNING POINT

Conferences played a major part in the development of the Helpline and ongoing volunteer education after we opened.

In 1985, during the Helpline's development stage, I received an invitation to a post-abortion conference in Techny Park, Illinois. I believe it was the first national post-abortion conference anywhere. The organizers must have gotten my name from my letters of inquiry to Youngstown, Ohio, St. Paul, Minnesota, and Pregnancy Aftermath Helpline in Milwaukee, Wisconsin. One hundred people attended this three-day conference. It was awesome.

There we were--one hundred people aware of post-abortion pain and wanting to do something to help people. There were lectures and ninety-nine other people to talk with and learn from. It was moving and exciting for me. These resources enriched our planning in every way.

Almost every year thereafter, I attended a post-abortion conference called **Healing Visions**. It was organized by Vicky Thorn and her staff at Project Rachel and the National Office of Post-Abortion Reconciliation and Healing, in Milwaukee, Wisconsin. Two conferences were at the University of Notre Dame, in South Bend, Indiana, and after that they were held at Marquette University, in Milwaukee.

Two other After Abortion Helpline volunteers went with me on different occasions.

During these two or three days at the conferences, we were submerged in post–abortion helping lectures, workshops, prayer services, Holy Mass and new friendships. The professionals who gave the talks were the foremost leaders in the U.S. and Canada. The participants were post-abortive women and men who were leaders of helping groups, and people like myself, trying to set up and run programs. We were from many faiths. These conferences were most vital and life-giving for me. I would absorb what I could, take notes, then bring this wealth of information and contacts back to our group.

At one conference my new friend, Paula Irvin, author of *Women Exploited* said: "Our post-abortive women who are here are so beautiful. And look what they've had to go through."

In 1986 at the first *Healing Visions* conference at Notre Dame University in Indiana, an astounding thing happened to me.

In my wallet, I carry a holy card image of the **Divine Mercy**. It is a picture that was inspired by Jesus Christ. Saint Faustina, a Polish nun, received a vision of this picture in her convent cell in Plock, Poland, while praying, on February 22, 1931. In my holy card picture of this image, Jesus is stepping through a closed wooden doorway, rounded at the top. Under this picture are the words: **JESUS I TRUST IN YOU**. I looked at this picture for years and drew strength from the words **JESUS I TRUST IN YOU**. At this *Healing Visions* conference, during a lecture by Sister Paula Vandegaer, I became very sad and weepy. I couldn't figure out what was wrong. I knew I needed someone to help me so I asked Sister Paula, this wonderful social worker sister, if she would talk and pray with me. I had heard Sister Paula speak in Providence in 1985 and I trusted her. Sister Paula agreed to help me.

We went to a room and began praying, thanking God and listening to Him. In a while I began to see in my mind's eye the picture of **The Divine Mercy** from the holy card. It came to life. Jesus was there smiling. Then I saw my mother appear through the doorway and stand next to Jesus looking very happy. In a short while my mother merged into Jesus and they disappeared. In their place was a great light shining under the threshold of the doorway. I sensed Jesus saying He was healing different rooms in my heart and would keep healing me.

I sat there serene and peaceful. My mother was safe with Jesus. I was so happy for her and so relieved. I always believed she was in heaven, but to see her with Jesus was so very good. This piece of my grief was complete. In the midst of healing after abortion lectures and activities, my grief was finished. I had been a child searching for my mother, and the post-abortion women and men are parents searching for their children.

REFERRALS

Part of developing the After Abortion Helpline was finding ways to share our post - abortion knowledge with the community - with professional therapists, clergy and ordinary people, friends.

One of our goals was to broaden our referral base to offer callers a choice of several names of professionals whom they could call for help. We also needed a geographical distribution of clergy and therapists to make it easier for people to get help.

We developed a referral packet containing these names and telephone numbers. In addition each volunteer had a Directory of Human Services Manual, published first by the United Way, then the Travelers Aid Society. Social services throughout the state including hospital numbers and After Abortion Helpline were listed there. We were also part of the United Way referral hot line.

In addition to statewide services we used another referral manual, a national post-abortion services directory published by the National Office of Post Abortion Reconciliation and Healing. They updated it periodically. If a caller needed help for someone in another part of the country, we could give them a name and number in that area.

This worked very well. I took a call from a Rhode Island woman who had a friend in California about whom she was concerned. Thanks to the manual, I had a name with a number for her to call near her friend's town in California.

Educating and enabling the public to help post-abortive women and men was important to us, so with the Diocese of Providence we put on a public "information seminar" on the evening of March 12, 1987 and a special day the next day for priests, to which Bishop Gelineau invited every priest in the Diocese.

About 100 people came to the evening program to hear three priests, an Ob-gyn doctor, two Helpline volunteers, a psychiatrist, and a woman tell of her post-abortion depression. Richard C. DuJardin, in a *Providence Journal* article on March 13, 1987, reported the following:

Diane Manning, one of the Helpline volunteers said: 'We're not professionals. We're ordinary people. Our role is to let people know that they can be forgiven, that they can forgive themselves and that certainly God will forgive them. And we do that mostly by listening to them.'

Dr. E. Joanne Angelo, a professor at Tufts University School of Medicine and a psychiatrist involved in a similar post-abortion program in Boston, said: 'Most women, after an abortion, will say they feel happy, relieved and act as if nothing has happened and this feeling can last for days, for weeks and even years. But then one day the denial begins to crumble.'

She said: 'Some women have attempted suicide the day their children were expected to be born, or on a future anniversary. Or the problems can arise in other ways - unexplained emotional depression, poor job performance or an escape through drugs, alcohol or promiscuity.'

'And one reason this happens,' she said, 'is that women have not been given permission to grieve. Quite often a woman who has had an abortion feels isolated and alone. She needs for someone to listen to her story. . . . She needs someone who will allow her to admit to herself that it was her child who had died. They need to share that with someone, so the child can be put to rest.'

The Rev. Michael T. Mannion, a campus minister at Glassboro (N.J.) State College, sounded the same theme, telling his audience . . . that if they are confronted with someone suffering guilt over an abortion, the most important thing they can do is listen and show God's love.

'We don't have to patronize her pain. We don't have to discount it. Nor should we over-dramatize it either,' he said. 'Condemnation accomplishes little, and may even obstruct the healing God has in store for her.'"

AT PEACE

At a Healing Visions Conference, a woman from the Diocese of New York gave out an article about a healing service called "At Peace With the Unborn." It sounded like a very beautiful healing service, something we might offer in Rhode Island. There was enough information in the article to plan a similar service in Rhode Island, which we did.

That same year, on October 18, 1989, we held a similar service in Providence, R.I. called **At Peace,** at St. Patrick's Church. We included those who had lost a child through sickness, an accident, or giving a child up for adoption. It was very beautiful. One woman who had several miscarriages was able to 'take care' of those babies for the first time and felt great peace from that. Seven priests were busy hearing confessions most of the evening.

Four years later, on October 20, 1993, we gave a similar program at St. Pius V Parish in Providence. It was called: **A Remembrance and Healing for the Loss of a Child**. Both parishes were centrally located in the capital city of this small state, so people from all over the state could come. We invited them through parish bulletins and newspaper ads. Those who wanted anonymity were pretty much able to have it.

As I write this, eighteen years later, we have given two more healing services at St. Pius Parish V Church in Providence. And our pastor wants it to become an annual event.

SECOND RHODE ISLAND CONFERENCE:

PERSPECTIVES ON THE AFTER ABORTION EXPERIENCE

We set our minds on presenting another conference in Rhode Island, similar to the national *Healing Visions* conferences we attended most years, so we could continue building a referral network for our callers throughout New England. We could not afford to do so ourselves. Fortunately, we applied for and were granted by the Roman Catholic Diocese of Providence an "Open Door Grant" of $6,400 to conduct two workshops; one to enable attendees to effectively help persons in their lives recover from an abortion experience; the second designed for priests, therapists, and volunteers.

Our New England conference was entitled, "**Perspectives on the After Abortion Experience.**" Vincent M. Rue, Ph.D., and Susan Stanford-Rue, Ph.D., co-directors of the Institute for Abortion Recovery and Research in Portsmouth, New Hampshire, were the principal speakers. It was held at Butler Hospital, Providence, R.I., on October 19, 1990.

On Thursday evening, Dr. Rue discussed "Abortion and the family: The Changing American Scene," and Dr. Stanford - Rue presented her own story, and spoke on "Healing the Trauma of Abortion." The evening program was directed toward the general public. The daylong program on Friday was for health care professionals, clergy and volunteers.

The following are some of the statements Dr. Vincent Rue made, as reported by Richard Dujardin in the Providence Journal – Bulletin, on Saturday, October 27, 1990:

"Abortion is not the safe procedure many people think it is, and it's responsible for many of the psychiatric disorders found among women."

"There are studies where the data is frightening, but these are never quoted by the American Psychological Association or the American Psychiatric Association. . . .They do not lead to the conclusions that these organizations want to hear."

" . . . [W]omen who described themselves as non-religious, or pro-choice, could be just as affected by abortion as women who considered it a sin."

" . . . [S]ociety's denial that there is something wrong with abortion makes it worse for many women, because the denial robs them of the opportunity to grieve and to come to terms with their feelings of loss."

". . . [I]n talking with women who feel anger or sorrow over an abortion, the key thing is to 'feel what they feel.' It's not to tell them abortion is okay. Because if we say that, we are telling them their pain is not legitimate."

The article also included the following:

"Dr. Irving Rosen, an associate professor of psychiatry at Brown University who directs the religion and psychiatry clinic at Butler Hospital, said his own involvement with the Helpline has led him to wonder if much of the depression and other problems experienced by patients at the hospital stem from unresolved turmoil over a long-ago abortion. He said he noticed that some patients with long histories of mental disturbance had disclosed to a counselor that they had an abortion many years ago and were still unable to forgive themselves. I don't know how extensive it is, but I believe that post-abortion syndrome does exist."

The article also reported that Susan Stanford-Rue shared her beautiful story which is complete in her book, *Will I Cry Tomorrow.*
It states:

"But she said her most important role is telling of her story and helping women move from pain and sorrow to the realization that if they can forgive themselves, they can also experience the forgiveness of God.

When the reality hits, the crying begins. . . . If you are in this kind of work, don't be afraid of tears. These tears are healing tears. The woman needs to know she can't be healed without the grief for the loss she didn't allow herself to have."

Chapter VII

OTHER PROGRAMS

Project Rachel

In 1998, *Project Rachel*, the Catholic outreach to women and men who are hurting from past abortions, was inaugurated in the Diocese of Providence. Its name comes from Jeremiah:

> *Rachel mourns her children; she refuses to be consoled because her children are no more. Thus says the Lord: Cease from your cries of mourning. Wipe the tears from your eyes. The sorrow you have shown will have its rewards. There is hope for your future. (Jeremiah 31: 15-17)*

In 1998 I applied for the part time job of coordinator of *Project Rachel* and was hired. Since I had been on the steering committee to develop it, I knew, if I was to become director, I couldn't run it and the After Abortion Helpline at the same time. When I was hired our AAH Board decided to suspend the Helpline for a time, and to offer our telephone helping volunteers' services to Project Rachel, which was similar to AAH, to keep the continuity of someone being available to help. Some volunteers were willing to do this. The Diocese agreed to pay for the phone number and the answering service, so volunteers continued to take calls in their own homes during the evening. The phone work was very similar to After Abortion Helpline work except we developed a more expanded priest referral list for callers.

During the day the Project Rachel phone rang in my office in the diocesan Office of Marriage and Family Life. The Project Rachel number was call-forwarded from the answering service in the morning when the office opened, and taken off call forwarding when it closed at 4:00 p.m. At 7:00 p.m. the answering service would call-forward the phone to the volunteer's home and take it off at 10:00 p.m. Although it was expensive, this phone set-up was the only way we could have evening volunteers, when most callers were home from work. Those of us who worked on After Abortion Helpline and Project Rachel believed it was critical to have a live person answer the phone, when a post-abortive person called for help during hours of service. It takes enormous courage to reach out for help, to make that call. That courage can dissipate if there is no one to talk to. My job was part-time so, during the day, when I was not in the office my co-workers, who had received post-abortion phone training, took calls.

A radio campaign was developed by the U.S. Bishops' Pro Life Secretariat in Washington and we received permission and funding from the diocese to run it in Rhode Island. It was a series of wonderful radio ads aimed at encouraging people to call Project Rachel. Tony Rizini, Office of Communications, Diocese of Providence, spread the ads out at key times during the day and evening. We received many calls as a result of these ads. I think fifteen people called the first week. The number of calls increased. It proved that if people wanted help and, if given a number, they would call.

In addition to maintaining the Project Rachel phone line, our first major task was planning a Priest's Training Day. Fr. Blair Raum, Ph.D., D.Min, Diocesan Program Director of *Project Rachel* Outreach, National Office of Post-Abortion Reconciliation and Healing, would be the main presenter.

In his letter to all priests in the Diocese, on March 6, 1998, Bishop

Robert Mulvee, Bishop of Providence wrote: "Since the central focus of Project Rachel is the Sacrament of Reconciliation, the success of the program will depend upon having priests throughout the Diocese who are prepared to nurture, support and reconcile individuals who are dealing with this sad reality in their lives."

On this Day many Catholic priests signed up to be confidential Project Rachel priests. In addition to this Priests Day, we held office hours and took calls, and we worked at advertising *Project Rachel.* In addition we gave talks at schools who invited us, and we visited post-abortive students who needed help.

RACHEL'S VINEYARD

On Saturday, May 15, 1999, I heard Dr. Theresa Burke, co-founder with her husband, Kevin Burke, of *Rachel's Vineyard Retreats,* speak for the first time and I knew I wanted to be a part of the post-abortion healing retreat that she was describing. The retreat was a condensed version of a fifteen-session model for groups, called **"RACHEL'S VINEYARD, A Psychological and Spiritual Journey of Post Abortion Healing,"** written by Theresa Burke and Barbara Cullen. The retreat sounded beautiful, and seemed to be a logical step in the progression of post abortion healing. I spoke with Theresa afterwards about the possibility of bringing *Rachel's Vineyard Retreats* to Rhode Island and she told me what to do.

Steve Burke, then my boss at the Office of Life and Family Ministry, also heard Theresa's talk. He agreed that we should pursue offering a clinical training seminar by Dr. Burke in Providence. On March 11, 2000, Dr. Theresa Burke came to Providence and gave a clinical training seminar entitled: The Healing Journey After Abortion. It was attended by interested lay persons, CP (crisis pregnancy center) workers, clergy, physicians, nurses, therapists and social workers who had an interest in this area. Continuing education units/credits were granted to professionals who needed them. The Diocese of Providence Office of Life and Family Ministry sponsored the day. Our office decided to build a Rachel's Vineyard retreat team that could offer the same service in Rhode Island. After many months of prayerful meeting, planning and training, we gave our first retreat on March 23-25, 2001. Each of us on the team of eight was deeply moved by the healing grace of God that flowed throughout the weekend. These retreats continue to be offered throughout the U.S., in forty-seven other countries, and in twenty nine languages.

TRANSITION

The diocesan *Vision Of Hope* capital campaign, initiated by Bishop Gelineau in the late 90s, funded a number of new projects, including Project Rachel. After Bishop Mulvee arrived he decided that the funding of new projects should be phased out because there would be no funds to continue them once the pledges, most of which were for three years, were fulfilled.

As a result, at some point in the year 2000 my part-time salary for coordinating Project Rachel was cut. We still had the phone system to do the work so I stayed on as a volunteer for several months. In early July our office moved from Elmwood Avenue to Stewart Street, to the basement of the Providence Visitor building.

There had been trouble setting up the Project Rachel telephone system in the Stewart Street office. It was very upsetting to find that our uninterrupted service had been compromised. On AAH and then on Project Rachel, we tried so hard to have continuous service. We almost always had a person answering the phone when we said we were on duty. On off hours we had a message for someone who called saying when we would be on duty. People could not leave messages. Confidentiality meant no one would know someone called. The person's name and number could not be traced.

This interruption of the Project Rachel phone system was serious and lasted for some weeks. I finally learned that allocation for the phone system had been cut. It turned out the three years of funding had come to an end. The office would keep Project Rachel but it would be staffed not by a group of volunteers but by a paid person already on the staff.

I moved my personal belongings out of the office and attended a nice farewell party given for me on September 12, 2001.

Our After Abortion Helpline group restored our telephone service for a short while. Then we ended our telephone service, though individually, to this day, we continue helping people recover from abortion where we can.

IF YOU WANT TO HELP A FRIEND

If you want to prepare yourself to help a friend who confides in you his or her abortion story, here are some suggestions.

1. Believe the truth that an abortion can be a traumatic, devastating experience, no matter what the reasons were, no matter who the person is, (male, female, teenager, middle-aged, Protestant, Jewish, Islamic), or when the abortion occurred.

   A mother who takes the life of her child runs counter to who she is. As the late Rev. Blair Raum used to say: "Mothers are always hard wired with three questions: where's my child? who's my child with? and is my child all right? A father's hard wiring is to protect his child. When he can't, he's devastated."

2. Know yourself well enough to be able to walk in another person's shoes for their sake.

3. Reverence the other person. Do not judge the other person. That's not our job. We are not God; we do not know their whole story or circumstances. We are to be loving, caring friends. Don't say things like, "get over it," or "you should be over that by now," or "get on with your life." Don't minimize their pain. Honor the reality that they are stuck in a very painful place, and have much painful work ahead of them to get free. Don't be the one who stops their healing process. Just be that Good Samaritan who helps them at this point on their

journey by being a loving, listening friend.

4. Learn enough about listening skills to trust that allowing a person to just talk and talk about a problem without interrupting them, or putting words in their mouths, or trying to solve their problem, can be a big help to them. Remember that as the person talks and hears what he or she is saying, connections are made interiorly, and some things become clear. They have answers within them.

   An exercise that helps one key into what good listening is goes like this: Close your eyes and think back to when someone really listened to you. Take the time to stay with that memory and think about how it felt. What did the other person do? What were you able to do? That memory will stay with you and help you give the same gift of listening to someone else.

5. Learn something about feelings and their degrees, such as anger, fear, and how people describe them, so you can reflect to the talker what they seem to be expressing. Example: "It sounds like you are very angry at so and so." This helps the talker name the feeling they expressed and acknowledge it. They might say: "Ok, yes, I am angry. I'm so angry I can't even deal with it."

The following "Vocabulary of Feelings," that can help you, is adapted from a University of Rhode Island handout I received from the Department Of Human Development, Counseling and Family studies for my counseling course. I have abbreviated it. This list describes a few different intensities of emotion.

THE VOCABULARY OF FEELINGS

Feeling		Level of Intensity:	
	Strong	Moderate	Mild
Happy	Thrilled, ecstatic,	Happy, wonderful, serene	Glad, good
Caring	Affection for, devoted to	Fond of, concern for	Warm toward, friendly
Depressed	Desolate, hopeless, despair	Upset, lost, discouraged, low	Unhappy, down, sad
Inadequate	Worthless, good for Nothing, helpless	Inadequate, Incompetent	Unsure of self, Weak
Fearful	Terrified, frightened, paralyzed	Afraid, scared, threatened, butterflies	Nervous, anxious, doubtful, on edge
Confused	Bewildered, in dilemma	Mixed-up, confused, going around in circles	Uncertain, unsure, undecided
Hurt	Crushed, destroyed, ruined, devastated	Hurt, shot down, criticized	Put down, taken for granted
Angry	Furious, enraged, burned up, bitter	Resentful, irritated, annoyed, mad	Uptight, disgusted, ticked off,
Lonely	Isolated, abandoned, forsaken, cut off	Lonely, estranged, alienated	Left out, excluded, lonesome, distant
Guilt - Shame	Sick at heart, unforgivable, horrible, mortified	Ashamed, guilty, remorseful	Regretful, wrong at fault embarrassed

Accept and respect the person and what he or she shares. Prepare to do so with knowledge of common after-affects of abortion. Educate yourself and prevent yourself from sounding shocked at something.

When we were on duty to take calls, we kept the following list in front of us. When talking with a caller it kept our minds clear so we could keep track of what the caller was saying. It also helped us listen well.

LIST OF POST-ABORTION REACTIONS

The most commonly expressed post-abortion reactions in order of frequency, going down all the columns from left to right:

NEED TO TALK	LOSS OF SELF ESTEEM	FAMILY PROBLEMS
GUILT	NO ONE TO TALK TO	SLEEP DISTURBANCE
SHAME	ISOLATION, LONELINESS	NIGHTMARES
FEAR	HELPLESSNESS	PSYCHOTIC REACT- IONS
ANXIETY	HOPELESSNESS	FEAR OF INFERTILITY
DEPRESSION	SUICIDAL THOUGHTS	HEALTH PROBLEMS
SENSE OF LOSS	SURPRISED AT OWN REACTIONS	CHANGE IN RELATIONSHIP WITH PARTNER
BETRAYAL	GOD IS PUNISHING ME	
SORROW, GRIEF	FLASHBACKS	CHANGE IN OTHER RELATIONSHIPS
ANGER	CONFUSION	
WEEPING	'LITTLE GHOST'	MARITAL PROBLEMS
REGRET	FEELING CONDEMNED	

Allow your friend to control the conversation's contents. Our Helpline calls were caller controlled. We stayed with our callers as long as they wished. Usually one hour was enough for them. But some hung right up, not able to talk. Or some became so overwhelmed as they talked, they couldn't go on, and hung up. Or another might have been crying so hard she hung up. The whole conversation might have been crying, sobbing and crying. To stay with someone when they are crying is helpful. It won't last forever. It is a response to deep pain.

Our friends will know when to end the conversation. We can trust they know when they are finished. On a first encounter of spilling/ pouring out the pain, there is a natural ending. The person becomes calm and appears ready to go on her/his way, relieved, strengthened and hopeful that their problems can be solved.

If appropriate, encourage your friend to seek a clergy person to talk with and perhaps a therapist for professional help.

JULIE

While I was writing this book, a young woman whom I will call Julie called me at my home. "My friend's Aunt Mary told me to talk with you. Can we get together today?"

"Do you want to see me because of the work I do?" I asked.

"Yes," she replied. We made a date for the next day.

Julie came to my house. She didn't know much about me, so to make her feel comfortable and to build trust between us I began to give her my credentials by telling my story. As I told her about Theresa Burke's eating disorder group, where most of the women had had abortions Julie said: "That's me," and she began to tell me her story. All that Julie told me was classic and is in the pages of this book. Her very serious problems began when she had a saline abortion as a teenager in another state, because her pregnancy was so far along. Julie delivered a well developed dead baby whom she never saw. She and her boyfriend, who was present in the labor room, never talked about it. Eventually they split up.

Julie turned to drugs and alcohol to mask the pain she felt. For many years this was how she tried to handle it. But by the grace of God she joined AA and has become a sober alcoholic. And now without the alcohol and drugs, Julie has begun dealing with the pain of her abortion. "I just want my child to be all right and to forgive me for the horrible thing I did. I killed my child. Is my child all right? Where is she? I think it's a girl but I never saw her. Is she with God?" Julie knew the Lord. She had been searching for Him for a long time. I told her that Pope John Paul II gave a special message to her in The Gospel of Life, and I read it to her. The message is printed at the beginning of this book.

Julie is a vivacious, kind, bright-eyed, lovely young woman. It is an honor and a blessing to know her.

FULL CIRCLE

The following prayer is from Mother Teresa of Calcutta. If you recall, it was in Mother Teresa of Calcutta's presence at my oldest son John's graduation from Harvard, on June 10, 1982, that I was inspired to connect with women and men who are suffering after abortion.

A Mother's Prayer
After Abortion

Mothers, pray, "Lord, My God, have mercy on me, for I have sinned by killing my own child through abortion. Forgive me, I will never do it again.

"But God, my Lord, my child is with You. For all eternity my child will live in Peace, Joy and Love. For the child is the most beautiful creation of your Love - my child being innocent. There was no sin in him. Forgive me, God. In your great mercy forgive me my sins."

My dear mothers, this brings you my blessing, Love and prayer for each one of you — that each one of you in your home will be a cause of joy to your family, that peace, joy and unity may always be in your home. Remember, the family that prays together stays together. You will Love each other as God Loves each one of you.

It is true, some of you have done the wrong thing in killing the unborn child in your womb - through abortion - but turn to God and say:

"My God, I am very sorry for killing my unborn child, please forgive me. I will never do it again." And God, being Our Loving Father, will forgive you. Never do it again, and believe me, God has forgiven you. Also remember your action does not harm the child. Your Little one is with God for all eternity. There is not such a thing that the child could punish you or your family. The child is with God. Your child loves you, has forgiven you, and is praying for you. He is with God and cannot do any harm except love you.

I am praying for you. I love you all because God loves you.

Mother Teresa
Missionaries of Charity
From a January, 1989 address by Mother Teresa to Japanese women who have had abortions.

EPILOGUE: A CALLING

A calling comes in whispers
    soft and loud.
A thought is heard,
    stands out among the rest.
It registers as "that makes sense to me"
    and then it comes again, eventually.
The birth has taken place.
    The thought is born.
Arrival brings excitement,
    joy's embrace.
For this wee thought
    has really long been known,
deep in the womb of God
    within my soul.

This whisper comes again
    it feels so good.
Its visit makes me warm
    I feel at home.
It brings together much of who I am
    and brings me to the fireside of love.

As I receive this whisper
    and embrace it when it comes,
it gathers other whispers
    that enlarge the very first one.
They're all pieces to a puzzle
    that my heart's been longing for.
The whispers are from God Himself
    inviting me, his child.

He knows me, He created me
    He formed me in the womb,
He's carried me along the way
    into this place I have no fear.
He knows my thoughts my life events
    my struggles and my pain,
Even when I stand or sit
    and what's inside my brain.

So we'll watch and see what happens
    as these thoughts start growing up.
Perhaps a tree to heal men's souls
    could grow from one wee thought.

JCP 11/26/86

Holy Mary, Mother of Mercy,
Pray for us.

Bibliography

Bachiochi, Erika, *The Cost of Choice: Women Evaluate the Impact of Abortion.* San Francisco, CA: Encounter Books, 2004.

Burke, Kevin, David Wemhoff and Marvin Stockwell, *Redeeming A Father's Heart: Men Share Powerful Stories of Abortion Loss and Recovery.* Bloomington, IN: Author House, 2007.

Burke, Theresa, with David C. Reardon, *Forbidden Grief: The Unspoken Pain of Abortion.* Springfield, IL: Acorn Books, 2002.

Catechism Of The Catholic Church, 2d ed., Washington DC: Libreria Editrice Vaticana, 1997.

Coyle, C.T., *Men and Abortion: A Path to Healing.* Niagara Falls, NY: Life Cycle Books, Ltd., 1999.

Edelman, Hope, *Motherless Daughters, The Legacy of Loss.* Reading, MA: Addison - Wesley Publishing Company, 1994.

Ervin, Paula, *Women Exploited.* Huntington, IN: Our Sunday Visitor Inc., 1985.

John Paul II, *Evangelium Vitae, The Gospel Of Life, Encyclical Letter.* Boston, Ma: Pauline Books and Media, 1995.

Kowalska, Saint Maria Faustina, *Diary, Divine Mercy In My Soul.* Stockbridge, MA: Marians of the Immaculate Conception, 2003.

Linn, Mary Jane, Dennis, and Matthew, *Healing the Dying.* Mahwah, NJ: Paulist Press, 1979.

Mannion, Michael T., *Abortion and Healing: A Cry to be Whole*. Kansas City, Mo: Sheed and Ward, 1986.

Noonan, Peggy, *Remembering A Spiritual Father*. New York, NY: Viking Penguin, 2005.

Powell, John, S.J., *Abortion, the Silent Holocaust*. Allen, TX: Argus Communications, 1981.

Reardon, David C., *Aborted Women: Silent No More*. Westchester, IL: Crossway Books, 1987.

Simpson, Eileen, *Orphans: Real and Imaginary*. New York, NY: New American Library, 1987.

Stanford-Rue, Susan M., *Will I Cry Tomorrow*. Fleming H. Revell, 1999.

The New American Bible, Catholic Publishers Inc., 1971.

Weigel, George, *Witness to Hope, The Biography of Pope John Paul II*. New York, NY: Harper Collins Publishers, 1999.

CPSIA information can be obtained at www.ICGtesting.com
Printed in the USA
LVOW111321060612

284921LV00001B/8/P